Spirit of the Village
A Maui Memoir

Jackie Pias Carlin

Write On Maui · Wailuku, Maui, Hawaii

Publisher's Cataloging-In-Publication Data
(Prepared by The Donohue Group, Inc.)

Carlin, Jackie Pias.
   Spirit of the village : a Maui memoir / Jackie Pias Carlin. -- Special ed.
   p. : ill. ; cm.
This anniversary edition commemorates the Filipino Centennial Celebration in
Hawaii.

   Includes bibliographical references.
   ISBN: 0-9772277-0-7

1. Carlin, Jackie Pias. 2. Filipino American women--Hawaii--Biography. 3.
Filipino American migrant agricultural laborers--Hawaii--Biography. 4.
Plantations--Hawaii--Maui--History. 5. Sugarcane industry--Hawaii--Maui--
History. 6. Hawaii--History--20th century. I. Title. II. Title: Biagan.

DU627.7.C37 C37 2006
996.9/0049921/092 B

Parts of this book were previously published in *Rosebud* August 2005 entitled,
Biagan.

Cover Design by the author
Cover Photo credits: author at 21 years old by Jon Petre
                                    author at two years old by Nagamine Studio
Text photos credits: unknown
Inside text photo credit: author in 2006 by Marcia Godinez

Printed in U.S.A.

Published by:
Write On Maui
Post Office Box 1210
Wailuku, Maui, Hawai'i 96793
http://writeonmaui.com

Acknowledgements

I could not have started or completed this book without friendship. These friends supported me in many ways while I began my journey as a writer: Chari Chalmers and Gary Landry, Mark and Marcia Paranada, Persis Hataria, and Dr. Gary, Edy, and Jackie Salenger.

Along the path, Gail Ainsworth, friend and historian insisted that I get this book published one way or the other. Marcia Godinez read the manuscript before it was really ready for eyes other than mine, and I thank her for being so kind. I also want to acknowledge Victor Pellegrino, UH Professor Emeritus, for his guidance as a writing instructor, mentor, and friend since 1966.

I appreciate the time that readers Phyleen Jackson, Bread Loafers Diane Crenshaw, Patricia Fox, Linda Healey and Clare Patton put aside for me out of their busy schedules; and especially to Puacita Hakela Carlin, Becky Kikumoto, Greg King, Tom Seif, and Carolyn Turner who read the manuscript in parts. I couldn't attempt this without Jill Engledow's example of determination, and Sky Barnhart Schual's positive words.

I also want to thank Carol and Dean Lem, authors of *Graphics-Master* for their afternoon of support when I was stalled at the computer. I also cannot forget Margaret and Joe Bowannie of Santa Fe, New Mexico when they delivered firewood after hours giving warmth to my soul when the temperature dipped too low for this island girl.

Jay Wilson and Shige Yamada created a cover that was too beautiful to use. Hence, I had to create my own cover, but not without priceless advice from David Barrett, Steve Hornbuckle, Marcia Godinez, Phyleen Jackson, Carol Lem, Bjorn Skrimstad, Angela Smith, and Cathy Torchiana. Gerard Gifford, Jake Hangartner, Jim Hylkema, Kris Nelson, and Bill Pray also responded to the question, "Is white print acceptable on a red background?" And Richard Fairclo and John Ching gave moral support throughout paddlers' morning coffee.

I thank my boss and good friend, Thomas F. Seif, PhD., of condosmaui.com, for allowing me time off from my day job. I am grateful for my aunt, Mrs. Leonora Artates, and for my stepmother, Manuela Pias. They have always loved me unconditionally. I am thankful for my breast friend, David Barrett, for his copious bear hugs.

For Puacita

My Little Flower

Spirit of the Village

The Camp

My first true love once said that I didn't know how to boil water. That stunned me for a moment because subconsciously I knew my future depended on whether or not I could find a husband. My father, Balbino Pias, said that after high school I should find a job and get married. Raising a family followed that. My boyfriend and I envisioned a basketball team.

Boiling water meant knowing how to cook. My father, although he didn't know that my boyfriend already had a concern about my cooking, decided to teach me. This happened around my last year in high school. We had recently moved in to our "new" old house across the street from the Pā'ia Gym on Baldwin Avenue.

"Come, I show you how to cook." he spoke in his broken Pidgin English and *Ilocano*, his dialect from the Philippines. He stood at the kitchen sink. I sauntered over to him and watched him. "Wash the rice first like dis. *Kirog* 'em wit your hand, like wen you cook fry rice. Den rinse it until da water all clear. Do dis about three times. Make sure da water stay clean. Den you add water up dis far." His fingertips touched the surface of the white rice and clear water reached midway between the first

1

and second creases of his fingers. The amount of water determined the consistency of the rice, whether it turned out wet or whether it turned out dry.

My father liked his rice a little moist, whereas my Auntie Nora and Uncle Aning liked theirs drier. Auntie Nora also soaked her rice a few hours before cooking so the dry kernels could absorb the water. My father didn't have the time to soak the rice after he came home from work. He was hungry. So when it was time to cook our staple, he added more water than she did. Her rice turned out fluffy while my father's turned out thick.

The finger measurement my father showed me was easy to follow. However, I was not always attentive to turning the heat down before all the water evaporated. The rice had to steam without burning. The smell of burnt rice attracted my attention as it traveled through the house and into the living room where I was sitting, either watching television or talking on the telephone.

My father did not cook when my mother was still with us. Before she left, though, the kitchen was the nucleus of our home.

When we lived in the old camp, Orpheum Village, my mother and I spent a lot of time in the kitchen while my father worked in the sugarcane plantation fields. I did my homework, ate my meals, and learned some handicrafts that she taught me at the kitchen table while she cooked. She also had our washing machine installed in the corner of the kitchen, between the stove and the sink, so she wouldn't have to walk outside to the back of our house to do our laundry in the *banyo*.

Over the stove, her collection of teapots sat on a shelf half as long as the wall. They were in solid colors — blue, yellow, red and green and of wide and bulbous shapes. They made my mornings very cheery. Hung across the windows above the sink was flower-patterned fabric that she gathered on a rod. They also matched the pleated panels that hid the space under the porcelain sink and wooden draining boards. Her cookbooks stood against each other on the first shelf above the kitchen table. Dinnerware and mixing bowls sat on the higher shelves, along with muffin tins and various shaped baking pans. Her Guardian Ware and casserole dishes were kept behind the pleated cloth panels under the sink. She was comfortable in her kitchen space. "Your mother loved to cook, you know!" my aunt would say.

In those days during the 50s, my mom and I spent a lot of time together. I followed her wherever she went. Once, when she hung our laundry on the clothesline in the back yard, I stepped underneath our raised house to quench my curiosity. I could walk under the house without bending; I was almost two feet tall then. Some travel trunks were stored there.

"What are you doing, Jackie?" my mother asked, draping a freshly washed sheet over the line.

"I'm looking." I answered.

"Looking for what?" She asked.

"Nutten," I answered, and shrugged my shoulders. "Nothing" was my usual response to a question if I didn't know the answer offhand.

"Well, go look for yourself. There's nothing there."

I continued my trip under the house. The empty space felt strange. A slight breeze moved through my hair. "Look out for the *obake!*" she called from the *banyo*. I hurried back to the yard and into the sunlight.

The floor plans of our houses were identical to each other, except for the porches that were sometimes screened or enclosed to make an additional bedroom. The houses were single wall construction. Our camp, or "village" as my mother liked to call it, had four parallel roads with approximately 12 houses on each side. The houses all faced the sugar mill about a mile from where our camp was. By the time I was born, the trees in the village were old, towering above tar papered roofs that sheltered our houses, chicken coops, dog houses and garages. Sounds moved through the neighborhood— rustling leaves, chirping sparrows, barking dogs, clucking chickens, crowing roosters, and shouting kids.

A huge irrigation pond lined with large boulders jutted up from the earth behind our camp. It stood like a volcano to me. Standing on the banks of the pond, I could see corrugated tin and tar paper roofs waffled between banana leaves, purple mango flowers, and the ever present *marrungay* branches with their long green and brown bean pods and fern-like circular leaves swaying in the wind. Our houses nestled under old mango trees that grew continuously from one yard to the other.

Car engines or motorcycles seldom rumbled through the camps although almost everyone had an automobile. Kids meandered to Nashiwa Bakery to catch the school buses or walked to our elementary schools up Baldwin Avenue. We attended either Pā'ia School or Holy Rosary School. When pineapple season started in the summer, the camp bustled with workers going to and from their day and night shifts around the clock. The women car pooled to the canneries and the men walked to the Bell House to catch the red work trucks that took them to the fields.

I lived in Orpheum Camp for the first sixteen years of my life, beginning in 1949. The village was primarily occupied by Filipinos (*Visayans* and *Ilocanos*) hired to work in Hawai'i, traveling from distant country-sides of the Philippines.

A paved main road separated our village from the Japanese camp, Nashiwa Camp, on the other side of ours. A small convenience store, Segundo's, was located in a central spot between our camps. There was a mix of ethnic merchandise that pleased both camps.

The store was not very large, maybe 20' x 20' at the most. Each morning, Mr. or Mrs. Nakamura, the proprietors, pushed opened, left and then right, the wooden accordion doors that shielded the yellowed walls of the interior. The foremost display was a glass hutch that held chocolates, rice candy *Tomo Ame*, waxed tubes of flavored drink, Cracker Jacks, Chinese seeds (cracked, whole-wet, and dry), and Maui Potato Chips.

"You like something?" Mrs. Nakamura asked whenever she saw me squatting low to admire the wonderful treats. I sneaked a glance at my mother. "No, not before dinnertime," my mother answered for me.

To the right of the store, stacks of local rubber slippers, Japanese wooden slippers, and Filipino leather slip-ons leaned on the glassed refrigerator that chilled fresh caught seafood. Bottles of *bagoong* were in line three rows deep on top of the refrigerator. Packages of dried *iriko*, *aramang* and *ebi* scented the room with the ocean aroma of what they were—gifts from the sea. Another refrigerator on the other side of the black cash register displayed fresh beef, pork and chicken for sale. Dried mung beans as well as other dried legumes, stacked in boxes, were displayed in front of that refrigerator, too.

In the center isle, cans of Spam, Vienna Sausage, corned beef, and tomato sauce were neatly stacked on the shelves. Open coolers stocked with fresh vegetables from nearby gardens and Upcountry farms lined the back and left side of the store. A big red cooler for sodas and a freezer for ice cream dominated the opposite corner of the store. These coolers were too close to the steps and hidden by the center shelves. I saw lots of goodies going into big handbags without the owners noticing. But the black cash register with the white numeral keys between the refrigerators never ceased ringing.

Mr. Nakamura prepared fresh *bagoong* at the sink behind the first cooler. He chopped off the heads, tails, and spines of *aku* and dropped them in gallon mayonnaise jars. Flooded with Hawaiian salt and water, the fish fermented in the tightly sealed jars and sat in the back storage room of his store. It was cool and airy back there and the concrete floors helped to keep the temperature right. When the fish was ready, he scooped full ladles into quart jars and put them on sale for $1.00 each. Our families were never out of fresh pink *bagoong*, the thick fish sauce we used in our Filipino dishes. It is the chunky forerunner of fish sauce or *patis*.

High in the back wall of the store, a long window with many square panes allowed the owners to look into the store from their living quarters. They seldom stood there, but one time I looked up and there was Mrs. Nakamura, peering through the window. Her eye glasses reflected the lights from the store. When she saw me stare back, she nodded her head and moved away. I heard the soft pitter-patter from her footsteps entering the store shortly after.

The store was shaded from the afternoon sun by a monkey pod tree that fanned its leafy branches over the hardened dirt. The dense earth cracked from the roots that bulged out of the ground. The roots reached toward the long concrete steps that met the width of the storefront.

People from the camps shopped here and some stopped to talk to each other. Sometimes a *luna* would stop and get a snack on his way to a field.

The situations surrounding me hinted that we Filipinos were treated differently. For instance, the roads through our camp were always in need of repair. My mother memorized the location of the potholes in our road so she could avoid them as she drove our car through the camp. I knew when a hole bugged her because she made a comment in her sarcastic tone. "When are they going to fix this road?" She was more apt to complain while my father was very private and did not openly complain about our conditions and way of life.

We bought fresh produce at Segundo's for our daily purposes, but when we needed weekly supplies or dry goods, we drove down Baldwin Avenue, past the post office across the street from the Pāʻia Mill, and into Pāʻia Town. Old train tracks divided Pāʻia into upper and lower. We thought it was better to live in Upper Pāʻia rather than Lower Pāʻia because of the smell that the irrigation pond below the mill gave off during harvest time. The odor of rotten eggs floated through the surrounding camps of Lower Pāʻia. I wondered how people tolerated the sulfur odor. It was all part of plantation living.

For a change of pace, we preferred Economy Store on Hāna Highway with its high grade meats and variety of fresh fish. We bought our clothes at Ikeda's on Baldwin Avenue. When payday arrived, my parents shopped at Kress Store or National Dollar in Wailuku. During the holidays, a giant fake Santa Claus stood in front of Kress Store. To me it was an overdose of lights behind pink plastic cheeks, a white beard and a red suit like pictures of Santa. I thought it was taller than a real person. I hid my face in mother's shoulders as she carried me into the store. Big places were scary. I was satisfied to be home in Pāʻia.

I used to think that certain people belonged to particular camps throughout Pāʻia, such as Honeymoon Camp, School Camp, Skill Camp and Hawaiian Camp. In my child's mind, honeymooners were very happy people, kissing each other endlessly, like in soap operas. (I didn't know anyone who lived there.) Ethnic mixes from Asia and Portugal lived in School Camp, and fair skinned people lived in Skill Camp. The fair skinned men were usually the *luna* or the boss overseeing the field workers. If I saw a Hawaiian person, I assumed that he/she lived in Hawaiian Camp, behind the Holy-Roller's Church on Baldwin Avenue. That's what my mother called that church. The parishioners sang, clapped and swayed in unison; unlike the parishioners in our church who stood, sat and knelt with strict reverence, while the choir sang in Latin in the loft above our heads.

Mommy (Rose) and me walking on the front walk.
The only streetlight in the camp is behind me.

Auntie Nora

Group photo in front of Auntie Nora's home in
Orpheum Village.

More Camps

The houses in the surrounding camps of Upper Pā'ia were similar to ours, except in Skill Village. Skill Village was below the theater where the houses were painted white and were twice the size of the ones we lived in. My fourth grade classmate invited me to her house one afternoon. I thought her living room was bigger than our whole house. Through the hallway, I saw a room with a shower, basin and an indoor toilet. I compared their facilities with mine: white people had indoor toilets and Asian people had outdoor toilets.

Her mother was very tall and had her hair in a braided bun. She wore a dress at home, unlike the women in my camp who wore mostly shorts or denim jeans. The women in my village wore dresses only on special occasions such as for church or parties. She poured some Kool Aid in glasses for us to drink at the coffee table in the living room. I wanted to walk into the bedrooms, but my classmate dissuaded me from doing so. At the coffee table, an issue of the National Geographic caught my attention. "Have you seen this magazine?" my friend asked. The pictures were amazingly colorful and the photographs of places I never heard of before amazed me. I asked if I could buy the magazine at Machida Drugs in Pāʻia. Her mother said I had to be a member to receive them through the mail. She offered to recommend my parents as potential members. She instructed me to ask my parents for the membership fee. When I did, my parents did not answer yes or no. A membership to the National Geographic Society was not a priority for my family, so I didn't pursue the matter further.

As children, we did not stroll carelessly into other camps or without good reason. Usually, I walked through Nashiwa Camp (where Japanese families lived) or Green Camp (where a mix of ethnic families lived) because it was the shorter walk to Holy Rosary School or Church. In our village, other people didn't have a reason to walk through our roads unless they visited someone they knew or attended the cockfights. If a person didn't know someone in Orpheum Camp, he/she would not know it existed. It was not visible from the main avenue, and the roads exited to the canefields or back to Baldwin Avenue.

The landmarks surrounding Orpheum Camp were Nashiwa Bakery and Pāʻia Gym. Across the street under large monkey pod trees, a one room building was a barber shop owned by a Japanese woman. The outside wall was stapled with large colorful posters advertising the Maui Theater movies. A Japanese Language School was next to it. It had tall concrete pillars on each side of the entrance, surrounded by an ocean-rock wall. I can hear the din of voices, even now, from the Japanese children who attended language classes after their classes at Pāʻia School.

Traveling on Baldwin Avenue from Nashiwa Bakery toward Makawao, more camps lined both sides of the street—Store Camp, School Camp and Nashiwa

Camp, to name a few. Haole koa and night blooming cereus covered the hillside on the right. Red hibiscus hedged the sidewalk on the left. My father thought that Pāʻia was the prettiest town on Maui at the time. At the edge of these camps and canefields, Pāʻia School and Holy Rosary Church and grade school occupied the landscape, one across the street from the other.

I observed the other camps especially when my cousin, Andy, and I walked through Nashiwa Camp on our way to Holy Rosary School. The front yards were very serene and the houses seemed quiet all the time, like their gardens, calm; each bush intentionally placed. There were a couple of exceptions, like my *hapa*-Japanese cousins' house where aesthetics were not foremost. Their front yard was contrastingly different from their neighbors. My cousins' cars were parked every which way in the frontyard, rubbish was strewn across their tall grass, and branches from their trees needed pruning. I suppose this disorganization came from the absence of their father, who long before I was born had contracted Hansen's Disease and lived in Kalaupapa, Molokaʻi for a while. When he returned, some of his fingers were deformed from the disease. His youngest daughter and I visited each other occasionally, crossing the ethnic boundaries that the older residents of these once segregated camps abided by. Her sisters and brothers were older than we were, in their later teens and twenties. Her mother was overweight and ate lots of white *tofu* covered with *shoyu* and chopped green onions. Sometimes she dropped cubes of *tofu* into her *miso* soup. My taste for these things did not develop until my adult years.

Their small living room was cluttered with Japanese dolls inside glass boxes that protected the elaborate brocaded costumes from the dust and grime blowing in from the fields. Lots of white ceramic cats stood side by side on a top shelf that almost reached the 10 foot high ceilings. They each had one paw raised while the other balanced on oblong Japanese coins. "What is dat fo'?" I asked my cousin. "Das fo' good luck, Stupid!" she answered. I imagined that they had lots of luck since they had so many of these ceramic figurines.

Unlike our *banyo*, they had an outhouse that they shared with a neighbor. The outhouse contained two separate areas each containing two wooden seats, paired on each side of one wall, and constantly ripening. The toilet paper, like ours at the time, consisted of rumpled newspaper or magazines, or rolls of toilet paper when it was affordable.

They took their baths in another room that was a separate building at the side of their house. It included a wooden *furo*, fueled by a wood fire. The family members took turns soaking in the hot tub after their showers. I could soak in it too but I had to wait until everyone had a chance to soak first. "Hot you know! Try feel da water!" My cousin warned me. Steam danced on the surface of the water.

Sometimes, she and I sneaked through their neighbor's garden to get to the other side of the camp, nearest the road that ran between our camps. The shaded garden was beautiful with various ferns and greenery. The narrow sidewalk was swept. A lantern sat strategically between the ferns. I was awed by the simplicity.

If our houses were built according to a certain grid, I suppose ours followed a sewer line.

In our camp, each family had their *banyos* in the backyard. Our *banyo* had a wooden toilet and shared one center wall with our neighbor's. If I timed it right, I could have my shower or bath at the same time as my friends did on the other side. We laughed, gossiped, or sang while the water from our showers ran over our bodies into a narrow gutter that trickled into a trough that led to an underground ditch. Our toilets didn't flush. Instead, a constant stream of water flowed in the ditch that our wooden toilets were built over. So on a good day, odors were nonexistent. On a bad day, my mother turned on the hose and let the water run into the ditch, rinsing whatever was clogged below. As a curious child, I often peered down the toilet to see what was there. The ditch was crudely formed with rock and concrete. Various items such as the red and white wrapper of a Lucky Strike pack, a feminine pad, or a torn letter could be seen floating to the ocean via that sewer line.

A sad incident occurred once when an unwanted baby was thrown into the toilet because the teenage mother didn't want the child. This happened in a camp nearby, but the news swept through our camp fast. Sometimes pets fell in and firemen came to rescue them. One day, my neighbor a few doors from us heard a sound coming from her toilet. She looked into the toilet and saw a male face staring back at her. She screamed and ran out of the *banyo*, calling for her parents. When the person of the face was confronted, he denied the incident. "Only God knows!" he said. I imagined half of his body under the toilet seat stretching to see the other side.

The shower head in our *banyo* dropped from pipes connected together to jut out of the wall. We weren't confined to a shower stall. The water ran onto the concrete floor and drained into the trough that bordered along the base of the walls of the *banyo*, and continued to the ditch under the raised wooden toilet. Next to the shower, faucets opened into double concrete sinks, which served as our wash basins where we brushed our teeth and washed our faces in the morning. One side of these sinks was also my bathtub when I was young enough to fit in it. As a child, I spent a lot of time daydreaming in this *banyo*, either sitting on the toilet watching dust particles float in a sunbeam through the four-paned window that faced our vegetable garden; or sitting in the tub of hot water, counting the drops that dripped from the spigot.

Our backyard also had a shed enclosed by chicken wire. It used to be a kennel for two boxers, Lucky and Brownie; but they were poisoned, my father said. A few steel wires stretched the length of the yard from steel pipe to steel pipe shaped like a "T" to dry clothes. My father's chicken coops took up the remaining area of the back yard, adjoining a patch of garden usually covered with sweet potato vines, eggplant, and other vegetables. A young guava tree spread its limbs wide enough for me to climb, while another old mango tree protected the garden from the afternoon sun. Behind us, the *Single Man* houses stretched all the way down to the Tournahauler road. The *pūnāwai* and the pond stood behind them. The pond was a huge gap separating our camp from Green Camp and the *Hongwanji* Mission.

A *Single Man* house (homes for men without families) was a series of single rooms that opened on to a porch built in front. The porch was U-shaped with about five rooms on each L-shaped side, and a hallway in the middle that led to the community kitchen in the rear. My Uncle Pimio moved into one of them after his divorce and when his children moved to O`ahu. The bedrooms were bare with only a bed and a dresser and a window. The community kitchen in back was built with uneven concrete floors and wooden walls the width of the house and separated from the main building. It was big enough for two or three stoves and refrigerators. My parents and I frequently had dinner with him since he liked to cook.

A Maui Memoir

We entered through the open hallway that was a boardwalk, and into the kitchen. My mother criticized his cooking because it was quite primitive. He cooked and served his tripe stew without cleaning the debris, and the head and feet of a hen or rooster often remained floating in his chicken soup. I loved him, though, because he always found time to talk to me.

There is more history to the *Single Man Road* than I know, but when I was about 12 years old, I joined my friend and her mother to a community bathhouse on *Single Man Road* where it had showers in both rooms and a big concrete tub in one. I could not distinguish whose side belonged to what gender because whenever we showered, someone had to be a "look-out" for the other. For that summer, I showered with them because it was different from my own *banyo* and I liked the company. We gossiped while we showered. I was also curious about that huge tub. It had a ledge inside along the walls that looked like a continuous seat. The tub measured about 6'x 4'. By the time I saw it, mildew and mold had grown into the crevices. I suppose it was used in earlier times, but we weren't about to scrub it to find out if it worked or not.

Although I doubt that this had any connection with the theater business that was called Orpheum Theaters during that era, we did have a profuse amount of talent living in our camp. From the first house on *Single Man Road* behind ours, I could hear *Tata* Posto strumming his banjo in the afternoons after work under his big avocado tree. Further down that road, another man owned the first violin that I ever saw. He made a yearning sound with his instrument, like crying. Across the road from us, another single man left his gold harp on the porch, sometimes playing it after his day's work in the fields.

Spirit of the Village

But they did not perform at parties like my father did. My father played in a string band that played dance music at weddings, birthdays and Filipino holidays. On Sundays they performed live over KMVI Radio. Promptly at 5:00 pm, A.B. Sevilla announced his Store Serenade Program in Filipino over the air waves. The red bulb above the studio door then illuminated, indicating that everyone was prohibited from entering. Sometimes I waited in the sitting room, peering through the thick glass window into the studio as my father and the rest of the band members played their mandolins, guitars and stand up bass. They even flew to O`ahu once and played on an all-island radio station during a Filipino Broadcast.

Our screened-in verandah at home was our music room. After his dusty day in the fields, Daddy brought out his Martin acoustic guitar and rehearsed whatever new sheet music he ordered from Music Sales in Wailuku. He sight read the black and white dots that meandered over lines of the musical score, and tapped his right foot to keep the tempo while he sang each name of the notes and in the right key. By the time I was in the first grade, I was already singing along with him and my mother. They encouraged me to sing solo after dinnertime to practice the songs I learned, *Dahil Sa Iyo* being the first one.

He also gave private music lessons to people. One of them was Joe Bulgo, an opera singer who sang all over the world. My father gave him saxophone lessons. (In 1978, I called Bulgo's Mortuary to assist with my late husband's arrangements. Mr. Bulgo remembered my father and told me how much he enjoyed their friendship).

Our home was immersed in music from the big band era and the latest hits of the '50s. Black 78 RPM records stood on their edges against each other in a wooden bookshelf in our verandah. My mother had another shelf decorated with a seashell made into a sailing ship and a photo of their wedding, both sitting on white, crocheted doilies. Part of the collection was my parents' recordings of their live performances at KMVI, including one in which my mother forgot the words and ended her song with laughter.

The music must have had lingering memories of livelier days, during the '40s, when they were younger, and the influx of military men invaded the streets of every town on the island. Military intercourse with the island women produced *hapa haole* kids that stirred beautiful mixtures of Asian, European, and Polynesian generations together. I wasn't one of them.

The *Black & White Orchestra* during a live
performance on KMVI's
A.B. Sevilla Store Serenade

My Baptism

Hānai

This is what I know of my past, from what was told to me and from what I recall through memory.

I was a result of an intimate meeting between a *Visayan* woman born in Hilo, Hawai`i, and an *Ilocano* man from the Philippines. She and her parents moved to Maui when she was a little girl. They settled in Orpheum Village. Her mother had many other children, but one day during WW II, my grandmother was sent to Kaneohe State Hospital after hearing a bomb explode at Kahului Harbor. Her mind snapped, and she laughed continuously until someone found her in her garden. After that, my grandfather was the sole caregiver for my biological mother, the oldest of two other sisters and three brothers. My grandmother lived at the hospital until her death in the mid '80s.

My biological mother was pretty at 17. I gathered that she was admired by many of the men in the camps. "Your mama, Jenny, nice *wāhine*, boy!" one man from the camp said to me when I was older. She became pregnant with me and married her lover. Things changed. Her new husband moved back to the Philippines first and she was to follow him.

I was six months old when she placed me in the care of Balbino and Rose Pias. From then on, I learned about my past in bits and pieces through photographs,

23

camp talk and what my *hānai* parents shared with me.
Whether or not there was truth to any of the stories I
heard, I never knew exactly what happened and why.

My Auntie Nora handed me a shoebox full of
photos one day in the late 1990s. It was loaded with black
& white and hand colored photos, dates scribbled on them
by my aunt or my *hānai* mother who was also one of my
many godmothers at my baptism. I found snapshots of my
biological mother, Jenny, in her white wedding dress, her
puffed front hidden by her flower bouquet she held in
front of her. My biological father smiled, showing a row of
perfect white teeth, black curly hair, and standing with
legs apart, the way sailors stay balanced on deck at sea.
She and he weren't standing too close together. Their
stance was void of the intimacy that lovers possess. In the
same box, wedding photos of other couples displayed
affection and happiness, couples cheek to cheek, and
smiling.

In another photo taken at my baptism, I am in
Jenny's arms when barely a few months old. Her eyes are
lost in thought. Or perhaps she was exhausted from
childbirth, as I was when my own child was born many
years later. My father stood next to her, wide-eyed and
smiling at the camera, but apart from her. My six
godmothers, including Rose, and seven godfathers
grouped together, shoulder to shoulder, and stood behind
us to pose for the photo. A statue of the Sacred Heart
stretched His arms above us all.

My first vivid memory was lying in a crib and
hearing two women arguing about my dirty diapers. I
opened my eyes and saw a naked light bulb at the end of
a braided cord hanging from the ceiling. The rest of the
room felt unfurnished. Later, my adolescent instinct

recognized that this was a room in my grandfather's house. As one story goes, my biological parents went to the Philippines, and my grandfather could not take care of me.

I was told that a big fight, with hair pulling, and nail scratching, ended the relationship between Jenny and Rose. Nothing much was said about my curly haired father.

As I grew up, I was frequently reminded that Mr. and Mrs. Balbino Pias brought me into their home when I was six months old. They were childless and having me as the new addition to their family seemed a welcomed decision. I called them "Mommy" and "Daddy" ever since I could speak.

They provided a "cushioned" life for me. My father always assisted me when I wanted to get off the *pune'e*. I was not allowed to fall. When my first walking steps came late, I was positioned against the full length mirror on the verandah wall to balance myself. If I lost my balance, my father gently leaned me back against it to strengthen my legs.

During those early years of my life, I thought our house #194 on the high corner of two roads crossing in Orpheum Village was the "center of it all," especially since we had the only street light in front of our house throughout the entire neighborhood. I felt we were special.

Other photos of my infancy do not exist after the baptism, but there were many after my second birthday.

I was shy and tiny, a finger constantly in my mouth—next to mommy, Rose, who was contrastingly larger than me. But I adored her.

In her teens, Mommy carried a lot of weight. Her round cheeks and bulky arms exposed her habit of over eating, but she dressed tastefully, accentuating fully developed breasts while at the same time covering her large upper arms with her fashionably crisp and ironed cotton dresses. Wavy hair accentuated her friendly face.

In a 1948 photo at Baldwin Park, where she is carrying one of her girlfriends on her shoulders through the surf, she is attractive and comfortable with her weight, laughing uncontrollably from the fun they are having. Her polka dot two piece bathing suit is a thin shirt, ends tied at her midriff and a short full skirt for the bottom. In another photo, she is posed on their rattan couch with Japanese motif covers on the cushions, gigantic blossoms in vases on the coffee and end tables, figurines of all sorts, and curtains with art deco leaf prints. The plantation house was full of island charm. Her house dress is starched and ironed, without a wrinkle.

She and Balbino had a formal wedding in 1946, she just out of high school. He was 18 years older than she. Their sepia wedding photo is full of thoughts of a promising future. On many of their earlier photos before and after their marriage, she wrote, *"Me and Honey"*.

My father dressed impeccably, too. Photos of him dressed in silk shirts and pleated trousers with a watch chain draping into a hip pocket are plentiful, taken as he strolled the streets of Honolulu. His hair is combed without a strand out of place, away from his forehead, reminding me of Desi Arnaz. In later years, his silk shirts hung snugly together in back of the closet, losing their place nearest the front. They gradually went out of style, but he kept all of them, including his numerous tweed jackets and blazers. I often speculated why he had so many of this type of clothing, especially since we lived in such a warm climate.

When I was old enough to ask, he told me he lived in Honolulu before he moved to Maui, and worked as a waiter in the hotels there. He must have had an adventurous nightlife because he once said to me, "...da *haole* ladies like take me out all da time."

Even in my teens, my father always dressed "to kill." His shirts and trousers were very tasteful and his socks matched his leather shoes that were always in the latest men's fashion. His demeanor was always formal in public, even when we had our lunch at Tasty Crust on a payday weekend or went shopping at the Kahului Shopping Center. His favorite dish was pork chops and Kula onions that he ate with style, slicing pieces of the chop with his knife.

He seldom wore shorts. When he did, he exposed his slender, pale and hairless legs. We teased him when he wore shorts at home, so he was more comfortable in long pants. My father's mannerisms were gentle, typical of Asian men.

Throughout his life, though, he seldom went out at night except to perform at parties, dances, or at the Royal Lahaina Hotel in the '60s, the only hotel in Ka`anapali at the time. He dreaded going to Lahaina because the old road in the '50s was "too close" to the edge of the *pali*, explaining, "...*bumbye* we get accident."

He was always cautious. My mother suggested that we take a ride to Lahaina one Sunday afternoon, to drive through the new tunnel. He hesitated, but eventually I was standing on the back seat of our cobalt blue '50s Oldsmobile, holding on to the leather back, anticipating the darkness in the tunnel that my mother prepared me for. My father blew the horn as he drove through it, like everyone else. When we approached the sunlight, my mother turned back to me and smiled, checking my expression, which must have mirrored some slight fear of the dark as well as the excitement about our long drive to Lahaina.

A Maui Memoir

The drive across the *pali* to Lahaina was my mother's favorite route. Descending the flat coast of Launiupoko, she would take a deep breath and say, "Oh, look how beautiful!" Traffic was nonexistent then. We considered it crowded if we met another car within 10 minutes on the way. But there were drivers who sped along the lonely highway too, especially at night. We lost a close family friend one late evening on his way home from the cockfights in Lahaina. He hit an oncoming car head on in Olowalu, as he overtook a slower car. He was dead at the scene, leaving his fighting birds in the trunk.

Uncle Aning experienced something unusual on the *pali*. Late at night, on the way home from the cockfights in Lahaina, he saw a woman walking on the side of the road and stopped to give her a ride. She sat in the back seat of the car and remained silent. As he turned a curve on the *pali*, he looked into his rearview mirror to get a glimpse of her, but she had disappeared. He thought it was The White Lady, Pele.

A trip to Lahaina meant wearing our best shoes and coordinating outfits. Actually, we dressed up whenever we left Pā'ia. My mother lost a lot of weight by then and abandoned dresses with sleeves. Her high heeled shoes had thin straps that accentuated thin ankles. Her purse and thin belt matched. She was now a slim young woman with wavy shoulder length hair. Every time she smiled, her eyes twinkled and her full lips parted to show exquisite and perfect teeth. She was a very beautiful woman. For me, those early years were pretty easygoing.

In those years, there were many afternoons when I pretended to be in a distant land playing out fairy tales between the lumpy roots of the shower tree that stood in front of the lawyer's office, across the street from where the Wailuku Library is today. My *hānai* parents attempted to legally adopt me, but Jenny resisted signing the necessary papers. They finally gave up the process of legal adoption. When the day came to register me for kindergarten at Holy Rosary School, they entered my last name as "Pias."

The first day of kindergarten tested my independence, or lack of it. My mother escorted me to the double door entrance of the sunny room, filled with animated paintings of Humpty Dumpty, Jack and Jill and other famous characters of nursery rhymes above the windows that faced the Holy Rosary Convent. Sister Ann Martin greeted us and took my hand into hers and led me to my seat. When I turned to glance at my mother standing at the door, she was gone. Then I freaked out. I eventually stopped crying, along with two other new students. What a traumatic experience it was to be in a room full of strange faces.

Another nun wrote our names on the blackboard and introduced everyone to each other. When she came to my name, she spelled it out: "J-a-c-q-u-e-l-i-n-e." She turned to the class and said, "That's such a *long* name for a little girl." I became self-conscious of that *very* long name.

Before Easter vacation, we were told to bring in some kind of plant to start a garden. My father poked holes in the bottom of a red coffee can, and then filled it with rich black dirt and buried a potato in it. I was so embarrassed when I brought it to school. I saw everyone else had store bought flower pots. I was the only one with a used red can.

When we returned to school after the vacation, vines were growing profusely out of my container. I didn't believe it was mine and was convinced that someone had

29

planted something else in my container. My self-consciousness was already developing into lack of self-worth.

My parents reminded me of my *hānai* situation very early in my childhood. They told me that my grandfather lived on the next road below us, and that my biological mother lived on Guam. The whereabouts of my biological father was somewhere in the Philippines, they said.

My *hānai* parents spoiled me. It seemed that whatever I wanted was given to me, within means, of course. I asked for a Shetland pony out of the Aldens catalog once, but that never arrived. Instead, we had a goat that was tied to one of the clothes line posts in the backyard. It had a short visit since it attempted to eat the laundry that my mom hung out to dry.

One year, a beautiful doll waited for me in a nicely wrapped box under the Christmas tree. With crystal blue eyes and blonde synthetic hair, it was the model of my fantasies, to be a child like that and with skin the color of the people I saw in picture books. (I can still smell her plastic skin.) The doll drank water from a bottle and wet its diapers immediately, as if female children were expected to be aware of this. But it was the dearest object to me. At bedtime, I propped it up in the box and laid it down next to the bed.

That Christmas night, we all slept together. As soon as we settled in, I heard a strange noise coming from outside. "Mommy," I whispered, "Who's mowing the lawn?" "Huh?" my father replied. I asked again, "Who stay mowing da lawn?" My father turned over. "No-bo-deh! Go sleep. Aieyy Apo!" he said. I fell asleep to the sound of what seemed like someone pushing a lawn mower somewhere under the starlight. I didn't know it then, but the sound came from the frogs around the *pūnāwai.*

My mother arranged my birthday parties at our house or at Baldwin Park. For one party, someone propped me up on a dresser and told me to sit still. Of course I could not. The dress hem pricked my skin and I was very uncomfortable. No wonder I had a scowl on my face. (A photo of me in this dress was printed in a 1951 issue of the *Maui News.*) Too bad they incorrectly listed me as "Josephine".

When I turned five years old, my mom invited my kindergarten classmates along with a few village children to our house for dinner. She made *chicken hekka* and served Maui hot dogs. At another birthday party, I received a huge top made of steel and painted with a carnival scene. A classmate who lived at the Children's Home above Holy Rosary at Sunnyside gave it to me. It wasn't new so it was my first experience with a recycled present. My mom overlooked it. So I did also. It became one of my best used toys. I imagined it was a flashlight that lit my way into dark and faraway caves, stepping on our *pune'e* that became high cliffs and climbed on to the cushions that stood in as boulders, guiding the (then) young and handsome Quinsaat brothers, whom I saw at parties. I didn't care that they were "old" like my parents.

I played with wooden blocks, board games, and paper dolls, everything for a single child. My mother also gave me a tea set. The pattern of beautiful red and green images could possibly have been from Alice In Wonderland, now that I think of it. I liked the clinking sound it made when I put the cup on the saucer. My mother included a set of play knives, forks and spoons that left a metallic taste on my tongue. But I did not know what to do with a tea set, so she poured water in the teapot and showed me how to pour some into each cup for a tea party. "But who's going to play with me? Will you?" I pouted. She took a sip from one of the teacups, and then placed it on the saucer. She brought my new doll over to sit in front of me. "Here, she can have tea with you," she said, and returned to the writing she was doing at the kitchen table.

My toy box was in the corner of the verandah, alongside the shelf of black '78s. I could lean up against the covered *pune'e* when I played, or stack its three rectangle cushions onto each other to add dimension to my play world. Under the *pune'e*, however, were boxes of surprises that taxed my imagination. Each box had a pair of my mother's high heeled shoes. One of my favorites was a red suede open-toed, strapped-at-the-ankle number with thick two inch high heels. I took this pair out of the box and wore them whenever she went outside to hang our laundry or when she was at work. My small feet only covered the front portion of the shoes. I stood in front of our floor length mirror and stared at myself, dreaming of the day when I would be able to wear shoes like those. Being the only child, I had many opportunities to daydream.

My cousin, Andy, and I were the only children in the camp without brothers and sisters. The best thing about that was that we didn't have to share our toys or space with siblings, except when we visited each other, which was almost daily.

He had a library of Golden Books. His mother arranged his books and toys in a small room next to their living room, walled off from the front porch. Before I could read, I was always at the bookshelf looking at them, turning the pages to see fire trucks that carried happy faced firemen, and a red smiling train that didn't mind the trek up a mountain.

Spirit of the Village

"Hey look, Jackie, the train is struggling to get up the mountain!" Andy pointed to the page. He quickly added, "But it's going to make it," when he saw the frown on my face. "Look. Turn the page."

Hānai parents,
Rose and Balbino Pias

Spirit of the Village

Birthday party at our house.
Andy, me, and Auntie Nora.
Mommy and Daddy.

A Maui Memoir

Small Kid Time

Tall, green sugar cane surrounded our homes as far as my eyes could see. Our camps were separated from one another until harvest time when the fields were completely burned and the clusters of wooden homes appeared naked against the red dirt. My father and the other men came home after work with dust-covered faces and clothing; only their eyes, protected by plastic goggles, were clean. Thoughts to themselves, they walked silently home on the dirt trail that started from the Bell House up to the stone wall that overlooked a basketball court and Cagasan's corn patch. One by one, they peeled off from the trail to roads that led to their homes. They were too tired to talk, or maybe bored, or possibly they missed their families in the Philippines.

Our house was on the corner, so I watched from our verandah for my father to head toward our driveway. I opened our screened door and stepped out on to the steps when I recognized him. I sat on the top step and waited for him until he reached the concrete landing at the bottom of the stairs. Sometimes he brought home a stick of sugarcane for me to chew on. Other days, he laid his *kau kau tin* wrapped in a denim bag on the last step. With a soft sigh, he sat down, bent over, and unlaced his leather working shoes.

Spirit of the Village

His regular shift began at 6:00 a.m. and ended at two in the afternoon. But in the summer months, the work schedule increased to 24 hours in the fields, with shift changes every eight to ten hours.

The harvest season was during the summer months, and my father's shifts changed every week. He was all right during his regular 6:00 a.m. to 2:00 p.m. shift. But as the shifts alternated weekly and around the clock, his energy decreased. His body and mind tried to keep up with the changing schedule. It was important for him that he had his full eight to ten hours of sleep through the heat of the day and through the noise from the neighborhood outside his bedroom.

My father seemed to like the "paternal care" the plantation offered. The plantation company provided homes and free water use. Once, my dad showed me our rent bill for the house—$14.00 a month. But when it was time for repairs, we waited for weeks to have plumbing done, or have the roads fixed. Our kitchen drain emptied out into the soil under the house because the pipe finally corroded. Our roads were rarely free from holes since they immediately reappeared even after black tar and gravel were poured into them.

A workman's strike occurred in 1958 for three months. Our food was rationed. A *luna* in a truck came through the camp and handed out canned goods once. After that, each family went to a designated "soup kitchen" to get their food. Our soup kitchen was at the Filipino Club House. At first, there was lots of food to go around. The cooks made *chop suey*, beef stew, or hearty soups. But soon, we were down to hot rice and salted cabbage. Having no clue about embarrassment or pride, I volunteered to stand in the soup kitchen line to get our share of food. Sometimes arguments would arise between the people in line and the cooks. Questions were asked about the amount of food portioned per family, and why foods weren't available other than just salted cabbage. Sometimes there wasn't enough food left for the people that were in the back of the line.

When the strike ended, my father and his fellow workers earned a little more money per hour plus added bonuses during harvest season.

Island sounds that floated through the air were muffled by the sugarcane fields by the time they reached our camp. Unike today, no traffic blared around us. No airplanes rumbled and no helicopters quivered above our heads. The only familiar sounds were the cranking of the Tournahaulers and cranes during harvest, the hissing from the mill as it exhaled steam, and the croaking of the frogs in the *pūnāwai*. Life was simple.

Once a month on the weekend after payday, we made a shopping trip to Kahului Shopping Center. My mom shopped at Ben Franklin Store to buy whatever she needed. It was also a time when I could shop like an adult. I could choose my own underwear—different colors for each day of the week. (I think that was her way of teaching me the days of the week.) She sized my socks by wrapping one around my fist and picked the right size T-shirt by wrapping the neckline around my neck. While she shopped for cosmetics and essentials, I shopped at the children's shelves lined with activity books and paper dolls. I was allowed one book or game on payday. When the craze hit Maui, I chose a hula hoop, a black one.

I spent many afternoons manipulating the hoop around my waist, standing and gyrating on the sidewalk in front of our house. At the annual cannery party held at Kalama Park, I joined the other kids in a contest to see who could do the most tricks with a hula hoop. Not being risky, I kept the hoop at my waist while others rotated theirs at their necks, arms, knees and ankles. Mine finally spiraled to the ground due to lack of momentum.

At home, my mother liked modernity so she filled our house with the latest appliances and furniture. We had the newest automatic washer while my aunt kept her old Maytag with the roller-type dryer. My aunt kept it for the longest time because she said "it wash mo' betta dan da new one." Every Saturday, I watched her pour bluing into the soapy water while a white load of sheets, towels and pillowcases agitated around each other. She mixed a drop of kerosene with Chinese starch to make my uncle's work clothes wrinkle free and shiny after she ironed them.

My mother also bought a new gas stove to replace our white kerosene one. She baked weekly because she now had an oven. Then our Zenith arrived.

We invited our neighbors into our living room to watch the test pattern fizz on the screen until the Kini Popo Show began. I thought, even then, that we were the first in the camp to buy a television. My mother liked to be the first person in the camp to try something different. She had the luxury to buy new things because she and my father both worked.

Some families lived in our camp for three generations. My mother and her siblings lived in our house before Balbino married her. Her mother died from childbirth and her older sister, my aunt, took care of the family of five when she was just ten years old. Once, I asked my aunt why she roasted a pig's head at Christmas and New Year's Eve. She said her father used to do an entire piglet over an open fire pit in their backyard when he was alive. My aunt continued the family tradition, using only the head, until cholesterol became a concern for her. The appetizing aroma of garlic and roasted meat flooded our nostrils as we walked into the kitchen after midnight Mass. Andy and I stood at the oven's door when she brought the roast out of the oven. Impatiently, we waited while she sliced off crisp, crunchy skin for each of us so we could dip it in ketchup and savor the flavor that burst in our mouths. I knew about my aunt's gastronomical talents from the time that I was very young.

My aunt quit the fourth grade to stay home and do the housework for her family after her mother died from childbirth. She returned to school a year later, but by that time, she had no desire for school. It was difficult to catch up. So she lied about her age and started working at the pineapple cannery. Still very young, my aunt married an older man. I saw him lay on the floor during the last days of his life so she could feed him comfortably. He was dying of kidney failure and there was no relief or cure for him then. Andy was only three years old.

When Andy's father died, he was buried next to my aunt and my mother's father in the Holy Rosary Catholic Cemetery. Still a young widow, my aunt remarried Juan, my uncle who loved chicken fights and ballroom dancing.

I often spent time with other families in the neighborhood. My immediate neighbors were a Filipino/Hawaiian family of seven children, and a Filipino/Puerto Rican family of five children. *Manang* Elizabeth was Hawaiian and *Manang* Minnie was Puerto Rican. Both married Filipino men. I visited their homes when my mother allowed me to. I ate whatever foods they offered me, too, such as poi fermenting in the poi bowl on *Manang* Elizabeth's table and *gandule* rice steaming on Manang Minnie's stove. Our cultures were diverse by this time, and I am fortunate to have had these influences. We were so intertwined that at first I thought that every recipe my mother made was Filipino. For instance, my mom prepared *bacalao* a lot. She soaked the dried codfish overnight and changed the water several times to rinse out the salt. After that she shredded it and dropped the pieces into a simmering sauce of onions, garlic and tomatoes. Later, I learned that this was a dish influenced by the Spanish. We also had the usual corned beef from the can, mixed with onions and fresh cabbage. *Bacalao* and corned beef were certainly not of Filipino origin but an influence from other cultures.

She prepared many authentic Filipino dishes, too. We ate *dinengdeng* practically every day. She paired vegetables according to taste and season. For instance, *marrungay* leaves went well with *cabatete*, and tomato and onions. We ate a lot of potato leaves seasoned with *bagoong* since the shoots flourished in our backyard. She prepared whatever was in our garden, or what was for sale at Segundo's. She liked using a lot of garlic in her dishes, pressing the cloves flat and sautéing them with the pork. Once I bit down on a whole piece of garlic and gagged from the taste. Fortunately, I grew to like garlic.

We shared food amongst neighbors in the village. If we weren't in someone else's garden picking lima beans from their vines or pinching bitter melon shoots from their patches, we were swapping soups or roasts. *Manang* Elizabeth gave us a whole leg of a baby pig one afternoon. They had just finished their slaughter and immediately brought a piece to us. However, the gratuitous offering was not accepted without my mother's speculation. She questioned why it was killed so soon. That question did not go well between my mother and *Manang* Elizabeth. *Manang* Elizabeth said my mother was too fussy, but I think my mother was concerned about sanitation and disease.

I may have been frail at a young age because my mother used to entice me with cool orange slices before

41

giving me a generous spoonful of cod liver oil. I can feel that warm, thick and unpalatable oil slide down my throat even as I write about it.

Slices of fresh papaya, straight from the tree were my midmorning snack, which I thought smelled like vomit when it was overripe. She didn't allow sugared snacks, especially not before meals. I was so well trained that when my second grade class had an Easter party at school one afternoon, I refused a chocolate bunny. The nun was quite stunned.

Parties were numerous in the village, especially if a family was large. Although *Manang* Elizabeth and *Manang* Minnie didn't host many parties, a family further down the road from us had at least one party practically every month. I tried not to miss these parties as the food was really good. Sometimes, a whole *kālua* pig was served, but most often Filipino dishes made up the menu. I didn't learn the Filipino names of each dish, but I certainly knew which ones I liked the most— pork pieces dipped in egg and deep fried, liver and pork stew, *pancit*, and fried chicken. Fried fish, as well as *'opihi*, octopus and *limu*—served when there was a good catch. *Manang* Minnie's husband helped with the food preparations and once I walked to their back yard with her daughter, Fely, and saw him and her brothers assisting him with a whole pig already slaughtered. He shaved off its remaining hair with a hand razor to eliminate the bristles. They worked quickly in the cool morning as the hot sun would spoil the fresh meat. I then recalled that in the dark hours of that same morning, its squealing alerted me that a party was about to happen that weekend. On many early dawns, especially during the holidays, squeals echoed through the village. But most of the time, morning sounds were the soft cooing of doves and raindrops from passing night showers.

Spirit of the Village

One morning, my mom suggested I put on my rubber boots and play outside. It was early. I could make out white clouds that reflected their shapes in the mud pools created by the potholes in the road. The water turned brown when I swept my boots across the bottom of the gravel hole. White clouds graced my reflection like a *haku lei* as I looked at my brown face in the still water. "Thock, thock, thock," a leaky faucet echoed in the shallow basin outside my neighbor's house, in which they cleaned their fish or *limu*. I stepped on their concrete slab path under their tamarind tree heavy with last night's rain. I walked toward their front door, hoping someone would come out to play.

"Hey, watchu doing?" It was Aggie from her kitchen window. I answered with a singsong, "Playing." The road was muddy and black from the wet gravel resembling smooth lava. It was the best time of the day. Plump fat clouds floated overhead touching manganese blue skies. Sparrows and doves called out to each other. Adults were still at their coffee cups.

We made games out of whatever was in reach. That day we picked the largest hibiscus leaves for play money. These were the $10.00 bills. The medium size ones were $5.00 and the smallest were $1.00. I stacked them in my palm, as many as I could hold between my thumb and fingers. The fresh leaves felt cool and smooth like soft leather, rinsed clean by the rain. Aggie set up a small store on their sidewalk. She sold rocks, rubber slippers, and guavas, whatever we could lift. Our activity lasted until one of us grew bored of the game. It was usually Aggie who found an excuse to leave me with a handful of hibiscus leaves and nothing to buy. When that happened, I returned to my own yard and climbed the steps into our house.

A Maui Memoir

Our front steps, made of wood, were wide enough for three adults to sit side by side. On either side of the stairs, bushes of white, red and pink begonias, flowers that resembled Queen's Lace, and tall green *tī* bordered the front of our home. They hid the gap of open space under the house. About seven steps led up to the front door. These steps were my "patio," my private place where I daydreamed or cut out figures from an Aldens catalog or fashion magazine, saving the pretty images in a shoe box. Sometimes, people visited. One visitor was a Caucasian woman, Ann Buffett, who visited with *Manang* Ingay, a cousin of one of my parents from Oʻahu. They stayed a week. *Manang* Ann showed me how to decorate a box with eucalyptus bark that we stripped off a tree on the way to Hāna. At home, she and I cut the pieces to decorate a small box, and we overlapped pieces with glue. I hoped to see her again after her vacation, but she never returned.

Our front steps welcomed people and hosted gatherings. One gathering in 1957 was for my Uncle Pimio.

I picked up the news of his death, prior to the wake and the funeral, when my parents contacted his children by telephone. They said that my uncle was admitted to the hospital and then passed away. The death wasn't explained to me directly, as I was too young to understand, they thought. Later on, my father asked me to draw a line on the edges of an envelope with my black crayon. He was mailing it to the Philippines and another one to his older brother, Thomas, in Seattle, Washington. He wasn't sure if they'd get the news; they were so far away. Uncle Thomas worked on a merchant marine ship out of Seattle, although he was a school teacher in his home country. My father had not seen him for over ten years. Being a child who should be seen and not heard, information passed over my head but trickled into my wide-opened ears. I learned that my uncle had kidney failure and was sent to the hospital, but it was too late.

We were in mourning. A black car arrived at the front of our house, and the suited driver opened the back doors of a stretched station wagon. Men from the camp, dressed in black shirts, pants and white gloves, solemnly pulled out a maroon fabric covered container with steel bars on either side. They grabbed hold of the bars and carried it into our house. The clouds overhead shaded the late morning sun as the casket they carried inside held my Uncle Pimio.

At the concrete landing on the ground level of the front steps, *Tata* Poro cleansed every person before they entered the house. Guava leaves and *romero* steeped in the *palanggana* of hot water, in which *Tata* wet his rough hands and washed my face to bless me before I entered my home. The living room furniture was rearranged for my uncle's casket. Candles smoked, making the humid day even stickier from the rain, people, and close quarters. Close to the casket, someone set up an altar with my uncle's photo, a lit candle, a shot of whiskey and a small plate of food. The atmosphere was heavy with urgency and loss.

Uncle Pimio's children flew in from all parts of Hawai'i. His daughter, Anita, with her husband, Chris, and their sons, Alan and Brian, traveled from Kauai. His son, Benny, his wife, Dolly, and their toddler daughter, Arlene, flew from O'ahu. Our house overflowed with people for seventy-two hours, from out of town, across the island, and down the road.

My father carried me in his arms so I could view my uncle. My first glance at the dead body was a little unnerving at first. His powdered face was stiff with death, unlike the smiling face that I saw the week before. A slight touch of rouge and lipstick gave him a life-like complexion, but the breathing human being was absent. He was dressed in a black jacket, a white dress shirt and tie, but I could not see the rest of his body that was hidden under the lower half of the casket. A rosary was entwined in his clasped fingers. I was glad to embrace my father's neck, to instinctively turn away from the corpse when my father took a step closer to the coffin.

Old and young people in the house recited the rosary together that evening. The adults knelt around the open casket. A crucifix lay on the crush satin that lined the insides, the smell of wax heated the room, and rosaries clicked in every female hand. A woman with a black lace veil, covering her head and face, wailed for a while. I knelt next to my father and my mother, and my knees hurt against the cold wooden floor.

I was relieved when the long prayers ended. Our tiny kitchen overflowed with people for hot coffee and Nashiwa Bakery sugar doughnuts. The collective sadness lifted as people drank and ate, talked and laughed. It was a party atmosphere now. Old friends rekindled relationships, some played cards, and others talked story. Arlene and I looked around for a card game we knew how to play. Someone slapped a *Hanafuda* card on to the floor. "*Yaku!*" another shouted. The gathering helped our attitudes. We laughed and wept together to allow the healing process proceed on its natural course.

At least one person had to sit with the corpse through the night. The rest of the immediate family and closer friends were stretched out everywhere, in all the beds, on all spaces on the floor, and on the *pune'e* in our screened-in porch. My father was fidgety. He wanted to be sure that someone kept vigil with my dead uncle in the living room. But my mother said that he was nervous because he was afraid of my uncle's ghost. Actually, I felt we were ALL afraid that his ghost might appear. After all, these were the same adults that told me that the spirit does not leave the earth right away. I finally fell asleep next to my parents, on the bedroom floor.

The next morning, I overheard the adults talking. *Manang* Elizabeth had seen my Uncle Pimio's ghost climbing out of *MY* bedroom window. I believed every word of it. My bedroom window was at the back corner of the house, closest to the *banyo*. *Manang* Elizabeth's bedroom, across our yards, faced mine. She must have had a perfect view.

We were very sad the next day when the hearse returned for the coffin from our house to deliver it to Holy Rosary for a Mass. A line formed outside our house and into our living room with people who wanted to pay their last respects. Everyone relayed some small message to him, either out loud or in their thoughts. Women kissed his forehead and men patted his hands.

All of a sudden, people shouted in confusion and men huddled over my cousin, Anita, who fainted in front of the casket as the men tried to carry it out of the house. I stayed home with Benny's wife and child as the procession of cars left our house. I was too young, my parents said, to witness the burial. My uncle is also buried at the Holy Rosary Catholic Cemetery, near the wall closest to the highway. My first experience with death was pretty dramatic.

Benny and Anita also grew up in Pā'ia before they moved off-island. They were at least 15-20 years older than me. They were frequently at our house after school when they lived on Maui. I looked forward to them coming over to the house, especially when Benny taught me how to jitterbug. I suppose the bug never left me because I still love to dance.

My aunt must have known that I loved dancing because she encouraged me to join a children's group that was practicing to perform for the Rizal Day Program in December. We practiced through the summer on Saturdays at the Filipino Club House. The other children who danced lived in Green camp above the pūnāwai. The girls, Lillian and Pauline, attended the same grade school I did and we were very Americanized, unlike the two boys who were our dancing partners. Casey and Johnny were brothers who had recently moved from the Philippines. Casey came to Holy Rosary, but Johnny went to Pāʻia School. Although we were all Filipino, the difference in our backgrounds was evident. They spoke oddly. Their accents were very thick with p's when they tried to pronounce f 's, and their habits were peculiar. They were very courteous to us and had gentle manners, unlike the cocky boys in the camp who were rough and acted tough. These two brothers walked with grace and kept their heads centered and high. I thought the brothers were *māhū,* but they were products of their Philippine Islands upbringing and just different from those of us born on Maui.

Our teacher was *Manang* Maggie Fuerte Ganutisi, and we were very obedient students. Our ages ranged from nine to eleven years old. We showed up for every practice and on time. Although we hated holding hands or being close to each other as partners, we managed to complete three dances. The names of those dances escape me, but they resembled waltzes and polkas. One afternoon after practice, we decided to walk on the Tournahauler Road, a shorter distance to their houses in Green Camp. I went along since it was still early in the afternoon. The girls and I gossiped about Casey and

Johnny. One of the girls said that Johnny had a crush on me. So I especially did not like Johnny. It's vague as to what started the clash, but out of the blue Johnny and I had a fist fight with each other on the sugarcane road. He let me swing at him, blocking himself with his raised palms in front of his face. Then his brother said it was time to quit. Johnny said, "I surrender!" Then he asked, "OK, can we be friends now?" So I agreed.

Their graciousness and demeanor puzzled me because they were gentle and kind, and not rugged and defensive.

When the evening came to perform, we dressed in traditional *Terno* gowns with the butterfly sleeves, and the boys wore their *Barong Tagalogs*. We danced on stage in front of the audience and the crowned royal court. I was so shy then, so I hardly looked at the audience and I didn't smile. However, my secret wish was to be in the royal court on the main floor of the clubhouse. Little did I know that this was just the beginning of my stage experience.

Every Filipino occasion had a queen residing over the festivities. If it wasn't traditional, it was made up, like the time the adults decided to add a Miss Pearl Harbor to the Rizal Day event. The two didn't coincide, but it didn't matter. Usually, the adults voted for the queen either by ticket sales or by good looks. During my days, it was good looks. That meant the queens were usually *mestiso*, with Euro-Asian features and especially fair skinned. I knew then that I didn't have a chance at a crown in my future. Nevertheless, I liked all the pomp and circumstance during the processional. A pre-recorded classical march filled the loudspeakers as the princesses in waiting and their escorts marched down the aisle through the audience that sat on long wooden benches. Then everyone stood and waited for the royal couple to appear. It was a fabulous event, moreso for the chosen queen as she was admired and catered to for the whole evening. The queen walked down the aisle in a formal white gown, complete with a sash and baton given to her to rule over the evening. After she reached her throne, she turned and presented herself to the audience. Everyone applauded, and applauded again when she was crowned with a rhinestone studded tiara. The scene reinforced my belief in fairy tales.

Ghosts, spirits and superstition were also major parts of my childhood thoughts. In fact, fantasy and reality intertwined quite often in our camp, especially for a gullible child like me. At one Halloween night, I was allowed to go trick o' treating with my *hānai* cousin and her girlfriends. They were at least five years older than I was, but it was okay for me to go with them that one time. I must have been eight or nine years old at the time.

"You be home by 7:30!" my mom said. "Or else the front door will be locked. You understand?" I nodded in reply and headed out the door with my Snow White mask and brown grocery bag for my expected goodies. That gave me an hour and a half to walk around the camp with the older girls. That was just fine. This was one of the few times that my mother allowed me to be out with other kids. My cousin picked me up and we headed down toward my grandfather's house. "Eh, we staying up until 11:00 o'clock you know. You goin' come with us?" she asked. "Why?" I said, "Wat for?" She looked down at me in amazement, "You dunno? Da witch going fly over da moon tonight and das wat time she come out. You neva know dat?" No, I didn't know that but I replied, "My mom said I have to be home by 7:30 but I can stay out, she not going do nothing." My cousin looked down at me and smiled, coyly.

Spirit of the Village

We visited a couple of houses and saw a few white sheeted ghosts running through frontyards. My palms were getting damp holding on to my paper sack half filled with candy and dimes. I heard her discussing something with her friends, keeping her voice down so I could not hear her. Then she turned to me, "Wait here, we going come right back." "Where you going?" I asked. "I wanna see the witch." She walked away with her friends, "Stay right there," she shouted back, as they disappeared behind some banana plants. I stood in the middle of the road next to my grandfather's hibiscus hedges as the kitchen lights from my house twinkled between the leaves. I waited. I looked up to the sky and saw a half moon rising up its course. No witch. The evening became quieter as the rest of the kids dispersed to their homes. Above the trees, stars dotted the blue violet sky, but still no witch. The cool Upcountry air settled over our camp. The gloom of getting home after 7:30 crept into my mind. "I going home," I thought to myself. I had no sense of time and my cousin had not returned. The streetlight guided my way as I climbed the wooden steps up to my front door.

I turned the smooth brass knob, but it wouldn't open the screen door. "Mommy!" I shouted. She answered from the warm kitchen, "What do you want?" With surprise I exclaimed, "I want to come in." She answered, "It's after 7:30 and what I said was going to happen!" I stood quietly, and remembered that the door would be locked if I wasn't home by 7:30. Oh boy. "And why are you late? Where's your cousin?" she questioned sternly. "I don't know where she went, she got lost I think. I . . . I wanted to see the witch."

My mom decided that the best witch viewing was right there, from the front steps of our house. In the meantime, the door was locked and I had no choice but to

51

sit. All my pleading and whining didn't work either. So I sat and didn't see a single witch flying over the moon. At 10:00 p.m., my father came home from his night shift and found me sitting on the top step leaning with my back against the front door. "Why, how come you stay here?" he looked at me with concern. I answered, "Because Mommy said."

I guess that evening the witch happened to be my mother.

Few and far between, one or two of the camp kids would be brave and come to our front door to ask me out to play. My mother told them to go home because I was busy doing my homework, exactly what she thought they ought to be doing also. Mingling with kids who lived up the road was not encouraged. I knew my immediate neighbors only, and my cousin, Andy. These were handpicked friends chosen by my mother, aside from my classmates at private school. Thus, if the other camp kids were outside playing peewee or softball on the road, they teased me whenever I walked pass their game on my way to the store and back. I was so shy that I couldn't look up to say hello or smile. I didn't have the knack of interaction. I became a loner, obedient and studious. My mother became the "mean lady," labeled by the village kids.

She did fill my closet with pretty dresses and matching patent leather shoes and frilly socks. I wore hats with ribbons. My bedroom was equipped with a blackboard and colored chalk. I had a bureau that unfolded into a desk out of the top drawer, with cubby holes for organization. My clothes were always cleaned and pressed, and hung on the door knob or laid out on my blue stool ready for the next day. I had E's for excellent in school and I was a very obedient child. I was so perfect that one night I dreamt that I wet the floor next to my toy box. I woke up and confessed, thinking it was real. She was sitting in the living room, writing. She asked me to show her where I did it, so I led her to the spot. She was upset when I couldn't find it and made me undo my toy box until I found it. Needless to say, it was just a dream and when I admitted it, I cried even more because I made her angry.

Choosing between right and wrong was sometimes not favorable. I gave my blue-eyed doll away to a little god-sister who had no toys at all. Her family's only furniture was three wooden benches in their living room. I thought my mother would be pleased with my decision, but she was again very upset. "We worked hard to buy that doll for you, Jackie." "Well, you can buy me another one." I answered. "No, I will not," she firmly contested. I was grounded through the weekend, as well.

To take the place of the doll, I chose a stiff giraffe from my toy box and took it to bed with me. I made believe it was my blue-eyed doll, but it had cold leathery skin and its body was not as cuddly as the doll's. When I asked for a Teddy Bear for Christmas, I didn't get it either.

While I played in the verandah, my mom was usually at the kitchen sink preparing meals, reading a magazine, or writing in her onion skin letter tablet in the living room, her cigarette balancing on the crystal ash tray on the mahogany coffee table. By this time she sold our old rattan furniture. She sold it for fifty dollars to *Manang* Elizabeth. Now we had a Philippine mahogany set etched with anthuriums carved into the arms of the chairs and matching end tables.

She only worked at the Maui Pineapple Cannery during the canning season, so she was home a lot. She decorated. The kitchen was painted a sunny yellow. The verandah, living room and corner bedroom took on mint green, and her bedroom and my father's extra bedroom had a soft sky blue applied to its walls. The walls of my room were the same as the kitchen. I complained, saying that I wanted my bedroom color like theirs, not yellow like the kitchen. But she insisted that it brightened up my room. I complained that it was left over paint from the kitchen.

She also rearranged our furniture more often than any mother I knew in our neighborhood. She arranged it to make room for another piece of furniture, but more than likely, she rearranged it to fit her moods. Sometimes she switched the chairs around to get the best lighting from the morning sun, to catch the breeze from the north window or when she wanted the best space for her thoughts. I woke up one night and saw her writing; the furniture had been switched around earlier. She used the arm of the mahogany couch for her desk. The tri-bulb floor lamp was lit behind her. I walked into the living room but kept my distance. "You changed the furniture, again." I said quietly. She kept writing but replied, "It's nicer this way." She looked up and smiled at me. "Go back to sleep now."

Summer was half way through when the pineapple cannery ran two shifts, morning and afternoon, 12 hours each. Now my mom worked full time. This gave me a chance to explore more of her things, graduating from her shoe boxes to her many shaped containers of cosmetics. Her vanity had the art deco lines of smooth corners and round edges. The handles mimicked alabaster, and the blond wood felt smooth under my fingers. Sometimes in the morning, I tiptoed lightly into her bedroom and watched her sleep. She slept on a big bed, under crisp white sheets and a spotless white bedspread. I sat on the cushioned bench that came with the vanity, admiring her shiny tubes of lipstick, wax pencils and various brushes that she arranged meticulously along the length of the large square mirror. I admired the homemade royal blue ruffled valance she made to frame the expansive mirror. A small white porcelain lamp with a frilly lampshade sat on the right side of the vanity. Her tissue box paralleled with the sky blue wall. Her hand mirror faced down and in the center; while the matching hairbrush and comb attended it, side by side. Everything had its place. If I picked up a silver tube of red lipstick and returned it ever so perfectly, she knew someone had moved it. Later that day, she asked me, "Were you in my room this morning?" I could not lie.

A cyst had formed under my left eye that summer. We placed hot compresses over my eye every day to bring the swelling down. When it did not, Dr. Mamoru Tofukuji scheduled an operation. My mother brought me to the Puʻunene Hospital on the morning that I was scheduled to undergo the surgery. The staff assigned me to a room with two boys and the nurses chuckled because they thought "Jackie" was a name for a boy. Instead of being privileged, I felt embarrassed. I didn't want to be different. But a friend from the camp, Edwin, was there too, to have his tonsils out that same day also.

My mom explained that she could not be there when I woke after the operation was completed. She had to get back home to rest and prepare for work. Edwin's mom would give me a ride home after the operation.

I was frightened when she left and kept my eyes on Edwin and his mother for as long as I could. A nurse came to take blood samples from me, but I refused to give her my hand. When she said it wouldn't hurt, I extended my hand to her. She pricked my middle finger with a needle. She lied. It did hurt. I cried because I was unsure what would happen to me next.

When it was time for my surgery, another nurse arrived with a white mask across her nose and mouth. She bent over me and I could see her eyes as she spoke. "Now, I'm going to put this mask over your nose and sprinkle some medicine on it so it will help you fall asleep. It won't hurt you." When I shook my head, "No," she said, "Oh, all right. Do you want to smell it first?" Well, smelling it first would be OK I thought. So I nodded, "OK." She laid the mask over my nose and mouth and placed a drop of liquid over it. At once it smelled fine and not too strong, but as the ether permeated through the mask it smelled of alcohol and bad air. I wanted fresh air and moved my head from side to side. She held her hand on my forehead to make me stop. As I struggled, it seemed that the ether fumes heightened and the odor affected my brain every time I took a breath. I groaned out loud. She held the mask in place so I could not take it away. I panicked but she kept repeating, "It's all right, it's all right." Soon I saw Sister St. Francis Bernard, a nun that taught fourth grade at school, spinning around in my head. Then more nuns appeared riding on that wheel too, all lying down with their heads touching, looking down at me from my head, laughing and having a swell time.

When I awoke, I still smelled that ghastly ether, and I felt a bandage taped over my left eye. I felt groggy and sick. I threw up. A nurse cleaned me and changed my sheets and gave me an aluminum bedpan to vomit in, if I needed to again. The odor from the bedpan made me sick. Everything smelled disgustingly bad. I was too ill to stay awake, and I wanted my mother.

We arrived at my house just as my mom was about to leave for work, dressed in her sky blue dress uniform, and putting her white socks and tennis shoes on for work. She thanked *Manang* Feliciana and the remainder of their conversation sounded like water bubbling down the sink. "Aggie and Theresa will stay with you tonight," I heard my mother say to me. "Just until we get home, ok?" I wanted her to stay home with me, not Aggie or Theresa. The bandage seemed to mask my discomfort and disappointment. I climbed into bed.

I must have slept through the afternoon. It was dark by the time I heard Aggie and Theresa come through my front door. "Hello Jackie, how you feeling?" Aggie asked. "Not good." I answered. "What time now?" I asked. "Around 8:00. We gotta go sleep. We get school tomorrow." Theresa added. I felt a little hungry but the girls weren't about to feed me now. They had their nightgowns on and they were ready for bed. "You hungry?" Theresa asked. I nodded. She walked toward the kitchen and I heard a pot settle on the stove. Meanwhile, in my bedroom Aggie plopped on the bed. "I like see your operation." Aggie whispered. "Show me." I leaned on my left elbow and lifted my body up onto the pillows to let her touch the tape on my forehead. Just as she reached for the tape, "Eh, what you doing? Leave her alone!" shouted Theresa as she peered at us from the kitchen. "I jus' like look," snubbed Aggie. Then she wrinkled her nose at me and sneered.

I was very uncomfortable that night. The three of us slept on my single bed. These two Hawaiian/Filipino teenagers had broad bones and firm flesh. I balanced my body on the edge of the bed. I thought of sleeping on the couch or on my parent's bed, but I was too obedient to do that. Besides, I felt too miserable to move. I felt worse the next morning.

Eventually, the ether wore off. The bandage stayed on for several days before Dr. Tofukuji examined it again. My imagination flowed freely. The last movie I saw on television was about a woman who went blind. After the doctors lifted the bandages off her eyes, she still could not see. As Dr. Tofukuji gently lifted the strips of plaster tape that covered the patch, he asked me to open my eye slowly, to get used to the light. I saw his kind face before me. I was not blind! Actually, not much had changed, except for a small scar under my left eye.

My mother felt I was now old enough to learn some new skills. One day, my mom flattened out a clean white dish towel with her palms, and laid it on the Formica dining table, those with the aluminum borders and matching chairs. With a green colored pencil, she drew a curved line diagonally across the piece of fabric, formerly a rice bag with its yellow logo bleached out. At one end she drew a small circle with five oblong shapes radiating from it. At the other end of the line, she drew two similar oblong shapes, one on each side. Then she threaded a needle with green thread and made three chain stitches on the green line.

"Here, you try it," as she handed the work to me. She showed me where to hold the fabric with my left hand and how to put the needle into the cloth without poking myself. First, I inserted the needle into the fabric and lifted the point again to draw it out on the top side of the fabric. Second, I pulled the entire length of the thread and laid it on the left of my first stitch. Then, I repeated the process but made sure the needle came out through the middle of the first stitch. I sewed this chain stitch over and over again until I was at the end of the green line. My sewing skills had started. I was proud of my stitches, long and puckered.

"You have to be neater than that, Jackie," taking the work from my hands and demonstrating the craft of embroidery once more. "Keep your stitches small and even," she said.

Spirit of the Village

Immediately, a shoe box turned into an embroidery kit filled with skeins of colors, a thimble, needles and a small scissors. I gradually went from homemade drawings to iron-on stencils. I embroidered designs for dish towels, one for each day of the week. I worked on pillow cases and every dishcloth that was white and blank. Soon there was no blank cloth left to embroider.

My mother never ran out of various arts and crafts for me to discover. I was learning skills that I would depend on later.

One of my birthday gifts was as a pink plastic book with a lock on it. A key was taped inside the cover and the pages were blank with blue lines printed on them. I must have looked puzzled because she said, "It's a diary. You can write anything you want in it. No one will see it." For the first few days, I tried to be loyal to my diary and wrote whatever came to mind about school or home. It was hard to think of real things to write about. Many days went by when the pages were wordless. Sometimes a brief, "Hello," Or "I don't know what to write," appeared on the pages.

I could not imagine myself writing endlessly like she did during her evenings by herself in the living room when my father worked the night shift. It was a while before I felt comfortable writing about my innermost feelings. I reread my entries from time to time, but did not recognize the value of journals except to record what I did that week.

To encourage my confidence in public, she would have ongoing conversations with me. Feedback on my part was minimal with the usual "Yes," "No," "I dunno" responses. Especially when we were in the car, when it was just the two of us, we'd have our short discussions. I was uncomfortable saying more than three words, since I knew I could be seen but not heard. One day she asked, "If someone asks where you live, what will you say?" I was to answer with more than one word. I shrugged my shoulders and answered, "I dunno." She corrected my sentence structure from pidgin to proper English. "Say, 'I live in Pā'ia', not 'I dunno'". Then she added, "If someone asks who you are, tell him you are my niece."

That afternoon, we drove to the Kahului Harbor and waited for someone she knew. We waited in the car for several minutes until a man in a navy uniform walked off the plank from a visiting military ship. She instructed me to climb over to the backseat. He came over to her side and slid next to her behind the wheel. He greeted her by her first name. He never once asked me where I lived, but he asked her if she was babysitting that day, and she replied, "Yes."

Mary Lanias Martin, Virginia Bermoy, and
Vicenta Lanias Andrade. Orpheum Camp Filipinas—
Before I was born

Uncle Aning (Juan Artates)
and Uncle 'Pimio (Eufemio Pias)

Me, *Manang* Ingay, Ann Buffett,
Mommy and Daddy

Mommy and I am standing in our front yard.
Papa's *banyo* in the background.
Road is between us and structure.

Surprises

"Where you went yesterday?" my father asked me. He was home from work and I was just about to leave the *banyo* when he blocked my exit. I stood at eye level with him, but I felt like he towered over me. "I don't know," I answered. I stepped aside and tried to squeeze between him and the door to leave, but he moved in front of me. "What you mean, you don't know? Where did you go?" I felt uncomfortable. An uneasy and unfamiliar feeling tingled in my upper arms and chest. I pushed the door to open it wider, but he held it in place. I let go of the latch.

I was suddenly afraid of my father, who was always gentle with me. His face was stern and I could feel his repressed anger wanting to emerge. I shrugged my shoulders. I whimpered, "Mommy said not to tell." "Tell me now, I said," my father demanded. "I dunno," I whispered, on the verge of crying. I stood with my back straight and my weight on both feet, but all the while I felt weak. We had been to the Kahului harbor. My mother had visited a man on board a navy ship. And I immediately knew that this was not good.

It was dark in the *banyo*. I wanted to run away. I didn't know who to protect from this new fear—my mother, my father, or myself. If anything went wrong, it would be because of me. Weeks, months, maybe years went by that hinted of my mother's infidelity. This was not the first confrontation in my family nucleus. I had been with her before when we visited her male friend. One of his daughters befriended me, and I followed her as we weaved in and out of shops in Pā'ia on Hāna Highway whenever my mother and I visited their home. We grabbed packages of dried squid for our snacks from one store where her mother worked, and then ran into her aunt's hair salon to eat them, hiding behind the dryers. We were never caught, thank goodness. While my mother visited with the man, his daughter taught me a hula, or we played jacks. Once we met at the Naska Pool. He and his children were already playing in the water when my mother and I arrived. I wasn't sure quite what was going on between them but it felt peculiar. That affair ended when he told my mother that he couldn't leave his family. Although my mother sounded very angry over the telephone when he told her, she acted as if nothing had happened to her emotionally.

By this time, my mother had lost all of her excess weight and had maintained a lovely figure. One night when we were home together and my father was on night shift, she tried on some outfits and asked me, "Do you think I look OK with this blouse on?" She had on a red sweater that showed off her shoulders if she pulled the sleeves down over her upper arms. I answered, "You look pretty, Mommy." She replied, "I didn't ask you if I was pretty, but thank you. What about the blouse, does it make me look fat?" I giggled and said, "You're not fat, Mommy." She paused to look at herself in the mirror. "Are we going someplace?" I asked her. She said, "No. Go to bed now." "Goodnight." I called from the bedroom.

I awoke late that evening feeling that something was not right again. My father was still at work and the house was quiet. I walked through the living room and into her bedroom, but she wasn't there. I called for her and when she didn't answer, I peeked out the window to the *banyo* from my bedroom. The lights were on, but she was not around. I panicked when I realized that I was alone. I ran to my father's bedroom where I slept that night, a habit I took on when he worked the night shift. My movement must have caused the head lamp on the head board to shut off because the room went black. I screamed and threw the sheets over my head. My crying and whining escalated into hiccupping and dry heaving. I cried myself to sleep. When my father came home in the morning, I told him what happened the night before. I was angry with her for not telling me that she was going somewhere.

Maybe everyone in the camp knew of my mother's escapades; my father was either very patient or denied it. Aggie and Theresa teased me whenever I went over to their house. My mother had found a second job working as a waitress at Hale Lava in Wailuku, and I spent the night with my neighbors when she and my father worked.

"Who she going see tonight, Jackie? How many boyfriends she get?" they teased. Craving for the attention, I exaggerated by counting them off with my fingers on my left hand. *Manang* Elizabeth scolded her daughters and told them to "mind their own business." Then she looked straight at me and said, "Don't talk about your mother like that. You no mo' shame?"

Aggie and Theresa did not have time to do the things I did at home such as sewing, playing with toys, or writing. Their spare time was filled with gathering food for their livestock of chickens in the backyard, and pigs and goats that they raised near Oma‘opio. Sometimes I watched them while they cut long grasses from wild fields to mix with the chicken feed, broke off branches of *haole koa* for the goats or stirred the boiling slop for their pigs. Most of the prep work was done in a lean-to shelter attached to their garage in their backyard. "Come Jackie, you like help?" asked Theresa, looking for an extra knife. "No, no let her cut grass. She too small. *Bumbye* she cut herself," their older sister, Ida, warned. They sat on small, short one-person benches, built close to the earth, cutting up the green leaves while the slop from neighbor's garbage pails, rotten avocados and other fruits cooked to boiling point to kill worms and other parasites. The container was a huge oil barrel over a wood burning fire. They worked side by side with their mother; the whole family giving a hand. Ida, who was the oldest, cooked, did the laundry and kept the house clean. The other children all had their specific chores to keep the household running smoothly.

One year was very bad for their family. Their father was diagnosed with tuberculosis and had to recuperate at Kula Sanitarium for a year. The neighbors, including my family, were also tested for TB. We did not have it. Once a month, *Manang* Elizabeth and her children packed lunches and took the long trip to Kula in the morning and did not return until evening. They spent the day with their father because he couldn't leave the hospital grounds. It was a hardship for all of them at first, but they got used to it. I wasn't allowed to join them. I felt lonely when they were gone for the day. When he returned home, he was very quiet and reserved, but he taught us how to weave mats from *lau hala* leaves. Weaving was a craft he learned while convalescing. *Manang* Elizabeth was so cautious about his condition that once while he slept she put a mirror under his nose to see if she could see the moisture from his breath.

Their home was always open to me. Each morning, someone unlatched their front door and swung it wide open to the porch wall, anchoring it with a rock to prevent it from slamming shut. The rattan furniture in the living room (which was once ours) was graced with white or yellow ginger blossoms fresh from their taro patches, alive with the richness of their perfume.

The family always made room for me at their wooden homemade dining table with wooden benches on each side. Since the family was so huge, they took turns eating at the table. I walked in one evening while Aggie was at the stove frying an egg for herself. Red Maui hotdogs were on the table. She turned around and asked me, "Would you like an egg? I'll make you one." I declined. My mother had told me never to eat at their house because there might not be enough to go around. But Aggie thought nothing of sharing her food with me.

I liked Aggie and Theresa and wanted to be everywhere they were. They were healthy, strong girls, while I was small and puny. Whether they had room or not, they managed to squeeze me into their old army jeep, whenever they drove from Pā'ia to tend their taro fields in Peahi. We'd ride a long way and *Manang* Elizabeth worried whether I had the patience to last the day. That morning my mother prepared my lunch of a boiled egg and some fruit. Someone gave me a pillow to sit on the corner of the metal floor of the open-sided jeep. We had at least seven people of different ages and sizes snuggled in this vehicle, along with tools and lunches. No one complained about the cramped situation. If it was up to them, the boys would have been hanging on the jeep's roof bows, riding up against the wind.

When we arrived, I was told to sit on a big boulder so I would not get mud on my clothes. As I sat and waited, *Manang* Elizabeth and her children walked through knee deep mud, pulling weeds between the taro plants. I watched crayfish swim between the rocks. Sunshine came through the plum trees above us and the water below me mirrored the puffy clouds that floated lazily behind the leaves of the trees. I wondered how good the mud might feel between my toes, but everyone was too cautious about my mother's reaction to see mud on my clothes, much less between my toes. I whined at least once, and *Manang* Elizabeth reprimanded me. I knew my patience waned early that day because I was not encouraged to join them again.

Manang Elizabeth was built like a tank. She could carry a huge burlap bag of taro weighing at least 60 pounds on her shoulder like it was a bag of laundry. She raised her family (including me when she had the chance) with strict and loving care. Each person had a chore to do and she organized them with ease. No one was ever idle, except at night when the family gathered in front of their television.

Their surplus army jeep was also their school transportation. Sometimes, Ida dropped Aggie off at Pā'ia School in the morning. On one particular day, sunrays struck the windshield of their jeep at a blind corner in Green Camp, just before the slight downhill turn to Holy Rosary Church. *Haole koa* blocked the view going around the corner. The glare prevented Ida from seeing what was in front of her and she crashed into an oncoming car. Ida escaped with some minor bruises, but Aggie flew through the windshield. She didn't come home from the hospital for what seemed to me like ages. I missed her and I though she might die.

After weeks in the hospital, Aggie came home with bandages across her face. She was cut terribly. The big gashes that ran through her cheeks, lips and forehead reminding my insolent mind of the monster movies I watched, particularly Frankenstein. She was very quiet when we walked to school together through Nashiwa Camp after she recovered. She crossed the street to Pa`ia Public School and I went a few feet further to Holy Rosary Catholic School through the parking lot in front of our church. My immediate thoughts were that she would have no friends at school with a face ruined from the scars that messed up her sweet face.

I was wrong. Aggie was chosen to be one of the school's cheerleaders and attended the track meets and other sports events. She was so busy with activities that our friendship grew apart. There was also the rivalry between our two competing schools, especially in sports. Our common interests were no longer shared, even though we were still neighbors.

Meanwhile, subdued tension grew heavy in our house. There were loud arguments with silence to follow. I didn't know whose side to be on. I stepped lightly through the house, hoping not to make a sound, fearing raised and angry voices. My parent's relationship weakened. We no longer ate together, my mother stayed in her bedroom when my father was home, and he hardly brought his guitar out to play. I loved both my parents but our world was cracking at its foundation.

Their relationship renewed for a short while, and our family seemed to take shape again. As if to acknowledge the renewal, my mother planned another family outing. This time, she arranged a trip to

71

Haleakalā to see the sunrise. My aunt and my cousin joined us.

The morning of the trip, we woke at 3:00 a.m. to prepare for the long ride to Haleakalā. My mother made coffee and hot chocolate and brought my sweaters to keep me warm. We packed my Uncle Pimio's old gray Plymouth with blankets and pillows. My mother and father sat in the front and the rest of us piled into the back. It was cold when we left Pa`ia and it was even colder when we reached the top of Hale-a-ka-lā. The leather car seats felt crisp and hard from the low temperature and the metal door knobs felt like ice. My sweaters weren't warm enough and I was pretty miserable. The wind whispered and seeped through the slits of the windows that we left slightly opened for fresh air. I didn't recognize the golden beauty of the sun when it rose above the bushels of pink and rose clouds that covered the crater. My arms ached from keeping them close to my body for warmth against the increasing winds.

We descended the parking lot as soon as the sun had cleared the rim of the crater. My mother volunteered to drive down, and I fell asleep by the time she made the third curve down the hill.

Suddenly my aunt began screaming, "Rose, Rose, what you doing?" As I opened my eyes, I saw my mother and father struggling with each other to take control of the wheel. The car weaved down the steep road, and my mother shouted, "We no mo' brakes. No mo' brakes!" My father pulled the wheel to the right. My mother pulled to the left. They struggled with each other to take control of the vehicle and to avoid the steep cliff on our left. The car headed toward the dirt embankment on the right and then gently fell over on its left side—its two right wheels in midair. My aunt and my cousin tumbled over me, our feet over our heads. "Mommy," I screamed. No one replied.

After what seemed like a long stretch of silence, I heard footsteps rush over to the car. "Are you OK in there?" someone asked. My father and mother moved around in the front, and we tried to upright ourselves in the back. "Here, take my hand," the voice said. My aunt crawled out through the passenger window first. Andy and I followed. My parents came out after. We sat on the white rocks on the side of the road until help arrived.

After the shock, my father was quite angry. He didn't speak the whole time we waited for the tow truck and for someone to give us a ride home. No one spoke as we sat on the side of the road. We felt pretty helpless. Later, my mother came over and asked me, "In the car, why did you call for me, Jackie? Why not your father?" I shrugged my shoulders. I did not have the emotional means to express what I felt inside at that age. I loved my father as equally as I loved her.

* * *

A Maui Memoir

"Is your mother coming to see me?" my 4th grade teacher asked. "This is the second time I've asked her to come and she hasn't responded." It was the start of the school day and my classmates were noisily getting to their seats. "Tell her to call me or else you won't be promoted!" she warned. I went home and told my mother.

Sister wanted to promote me into the fifth grade in the middle of the year. She felt that I showed potential to benefit at a higher level. My mother agreed. The next week I was in the midst of 5th graders and a new teacher. After the 5th grade teacher introduced me to her class, she exclaimed "Well, we'll see how smart you are!" with more than a hint of sarcasm. All of a sudden, I felt very, very small. I was not up for the challenge.

I wished I were invisible.

My tiny physique was not enough to shroud the confusion that grew inside me. I prepared for school one morning while my mother remained extremely quiet. She wrapped her blue chenille bathrobe closer to her body while she placed my breakfast of toast and cocoa in front of me. A frown burrowed between her eyes as she pulled a chair away from the table and sat down. "You be a good girl, you understand?" she said to me. I nodded. "Listen to your father and help him, ok?" she asked. I said, "Ok," although I did not quite know exactly what I was agreeing to. I always helped him by picking up the stray leaves when he raked them into a pile before he burned them. I loved to watch the embers grow yellow and orange between the black embers, a miniature cane fire. I sang along with him every time he called on me to sing. Nothing else was asked of me then. So helping him now was not a clear request to me. She handed me my books and hugged me. I walked down our front steps.

Spirit of the Village

I was puzzled by her manner as I left our driveway. I walked a little further and then turned around and saw her standing at the front door, watching me as I walked away. It was something she never did before. When I returned home from school that afternoon, the air was buzzing with confusion and anger. My aunt and my father shouted and blamed each other for something that apparently happened that morning. I stood beside them in the front yard while they decided on who was to go to the airport to pick up our car. The croton bushes blocked my view of them arguing. My sense of being shrank to minuteness. "I can go, too?" I asked when they were ready to go. "No, you stay home," someone said. "Where's Mommy?" I asked. "She ran away," a voice said.

Ran away? I had an idea of what that meant. Many women and children "ran away" from home. My biological mother did. Now my *hānai* mother was running too?

I turned away as the car moved from our driveway. I walked to our *banyo*. The sun and sky were neutral to my blank thoughts. I touched the wall of our house, feeling the roughness of the weathered wood with my fingertips. I drew an imaginary line across the entire length of the house with my forefinger, being careful not to lose my balance on the loose concrete steps in the pathway. The *banyo* was a safe place to go as thoughts rushed bumper to bumper in my mind. When will she come back? Maybe she went to meet someone at the airport. Did somebody steal our car? I reached the *banyo* and waited for my eyes to adjust to the darkness inside. Our three white bath towels hung from the wire line, each one in its rightful place. I intended to sit on the toilet and daydream, my usual reaction when I had idle time and I didn't know what else to do. But instead I reached for her towel and held it between my hands. I placed my face in her towel for comfort. I felt lost and empty, but her scent that was left on the towel engulfed me. My eyes burned as I tried to prevent myself from crying. I know now that what I was feeling was the helpless grief of abandonment.

Our flowering plants of multicolored begonias and white pompoms between sturdy Hawaiian ferns soon died around the perimeters of the house, leaving only brown scraggy stems stretching out from the dry dirt. The concrete sidewalk was stained brown from the neglect of whitewash scrubbing that she managed to have time for every weekend. The rose bushes once filled with pink and red blossoms now failed to bloom.

The stronger plants that did not need constant nurturing—the coconut tree that grew beside our driveway, the mango tree that shaded the garage, and the avocado tree along the road, spread their roots to the nearest source of underground water. They were here to stay. Our red *ti* that grew along our sidewalk that led to the *banyo* managed to survive because of *Manang* Elizabeth's far reaching lawn sprinkler. Fleas bred in crevices of our *banyo* floor and multiplied in the dried up backyard. Summer was coming. The rest of my 5th grade was grueling. Besides wrestling with my loss and grief, studying was difficult. The 5th grade teacher's system of privilege was allowing the top student with the highest average of the week to sit at the assigned first desk in front of the class, and every child sat consecutively according to their average grade after that. I began the day with a seat very close to the front of the class. But by the end of the day, scores changed dramatically. I could not get a grip on math and every Friday after our tests, I sat in one of the last seats of the room.

I couldn't wait for 5th grade to end. When summer vacation arrived, our boring days were exaggerated by the lack of activities while our parents worked. So Andy and I used our imaginations. We sat in our "cockpits" that were my grandfather's hibiscus hedges —lean, tall, thirsty, and unattended—that grew over our heads. Despite their sparseness, they were strong enough to hold our little bodies. Andrew climbed one bush and I took another beside him. The supple branches swayed under our weight as we held on to the ones above us to avoid from falling. Balancing ourselves, we sat between forks of branches, and our feet nestled in between the knots. The instrument panel was made up of more leaves, branches and hibiscus. We sat only a few feet from the ground, but above us the cloudless sky was our ceiling. As we sat in our seats, my daydreams were of my mother. Andy soared through the air, imagining the earth below him. He was encouraged to dream. He built model airplanes that hung from his bedroom ceiling. He displayed his favorite jet on his bureau. I tried building a model airplane once, too. I did not have the patience to wait for the glue to harden. I eventually gave the unfinished model to him to complete. Our airplanes faded away when my grandfather decided to trim his hedges. I turned to books and read a lot of fairy tales.

As with everything, when one door closes another one opens.

* * *

Photo taken in 1959 -
Me and our 1957 Oldsmobile

Jenny as a young teenager
in Orpheum Camp

I was coming out of my aunt's *banyo* as my grandfather was going into his. He and my aunt's *banyos* shared the same roof. "What you doing, *'Dai?*" He always called me '*Dai*, short for *"Inday,"* the word for a young lady. "Nothing." I said. We spoke over the kerosene gallon drum that sat on wooden two-by-fours, crisscrossed at both ends. He took off his eyeglasses and cleaned them with the tail of his shirt. He wiped his balding head with the back of his arm and placed his glasses back on. His clothes weren't dusty from the fields since he worked in the mill.

"You like see your mama?" he asked, tentatively but surely. Stunned, I didn't answer. Finding my voice, I murmured, "Which mama?" He nodded and looked at me, "Your real one." I thought of the repercussions from my aunt and father if I agreed to see her. Mention of her name or questions about her were not encouraged.

I was told that she didn't want me.

He must have sensed my hesitation, and offered further, "You come my house wen you get time. I show you her pitcha." I said, "OK."

"Papa!" I called out. "Papa!" My grandfather answered from his enclosed porch. "Come inside, 'Dai." The porch was dimly lit by the afternoon sun. The windows in the porch were smaller than ours and were covered with curtains. But in contrast, the living room was full of sunshine. Framed photographs hung on the wall. One was of his son, Johnny, posed with his boxing gloves, and another was my grandfather with my grandmother in a formal shot when they were younger.

The sparse room had a brown rattan couch without cushions, situated in front of a window that faced his backyard. A black Singer sewing machine stood diagonally forlorn against one corner. I returned my focus to my grandfather in the semi-darkness. I saw him sitting in a homemade wooden chair, with adjustments that brought the back forward or backward. He had his feet up, relaxing. "Wow," I said, "I neva saw one chair like dat before." He laughed.

Smoke curled from his pipe as he inhaled his tobacco; the room smelled sweet from the smoke. On a shelf under the window, a circular wooden rack held his various pipes and a can of tobacco had its place near his reach. A small bronze spittoon sat on the floor beside him. This was the first time I visited my grandfather alone.

The only other encounters I had with him were during Christmas or my birthday when he gave me dimes as presents. There were times he waited for me on his porch steps as I walked to my aunt's house or when Andy and I played in his large front yard under the monkey pod tree. I also visited him when his older children returned from where they lived off island; *Manang* Sising, *Manong* Willie or *Manong* Johnny. He also had two younger children. Robert lived with him and attended St. Anthony Boys School until he graduated, and then left Maui when he joined a seminary. His youngest child, Rosina, lived with another family in Lower Pa'ia.

One time, he came to our house with a pair of parakeets and asked my mother if I could have them. She accepted them, but after he left she remarked that they were something else he didn't want. I instinctively felt that the other unwanted "else" was in reference to me.

But now I felt warmer toward him, without my *hānai* mother to influence my thoughts. He got up from his chair and I followed him across the kitchen into his corner room. The sparse kitchen had a checkered oil cloth over a square dining table accompanied by two wooden chairs. Over his white stove, a jar of Postum sat on a shelf with a box of salt and a can of pepper. His kitchen counter bowed a little in the middle where it held up the porcelain sink. The linoleum on the floor was faded and cracked at the edges. A pair of yellowed curtains covered the entrance to another room. The smell of stale tobacco lingered in the air.

I followed him into a corner bedroom beyond the kitchen, small enough for a single bed, a desk and a chair. Army blankets hung across the two narrow windows. They made the room very dark. It never occurred to me then that these blankets might have been left there since WW II. A black typewriter sat alone on the desktop, and my eyes immediately widened.

I asked, "Can I type?" "You type?" he asked.

"No, but I like try." I answered. He took two sheets of paper out from one of the drawers and rolled them into the carriage. "You practice," he said. I saw typewriters before but didn't actually get to use one until then. I was impressed with the keys that could print the alphabet on paper by pressing them with my fingers. While I pressed the keys one at a time, he rummaged through some letters that he had on a shelf behind me. He opened one of them and handed me a photograph.

The young woman in the photo was leaning against a palm tree, one foot up against the trunk, her knee pointed to the camera. Her hands were tucked behind her back. Her short hair framed her soft face and a slight grin graced her features. "This is Jenny, your real mother," my grandfather told me. I took a deep breath and held the photograph between my fingers. My immediate reaction was relief. I still had hope for someone to call my own.

"You write her one letter," my grandfather suggested. My mind brightened up, "Oh, I can type her one letta!" He smiled at my eagerness and allowed me to begin my first communication with her.

I rolled two sheets of white paper into the carriage like he showed me previously. "D-e-a-r M-o-m," I typed. Then I moved the carriage return. Click, click, click went the keys. If I didn't press the key hard enough, the letter came out gray rather than black. Searching for each letter took longer than I expected since I did not know where all the keys were located in each row. After about five minutes, I became bored with the time it took to type out the sentences that were forming in my mind. Discouraged, I turned around and told my grandfather that I would have to finish writing it in long hand at home. I also did not know what to say in the letter. "Papa, what should I say?" I asked. He said, "Introduce yourself, tell her I said to write to you, and then ask her to send money."

When I finished the letter, I brought it over to him to read and he liked what I wrote. He obviously mailed it because three weeks later, a letter arrived.

My aunt was beside herself. "Why you write to her? Who told you to write to her?" I answered as best as I could. I wanted to know who my real mother was and Papa suggested that I write to her. The incident was not discussed again and our correspondence ended. The summer wore on.

Heaven must have intervened because the rest of the summer was filled with new activities. Pastor Edward Dodd, a new Baptist minister on Maui, drove a white van to the middle of the camp next to the stone wall above the basketball court built behind the Bell House. The van was parked there until his word spread throughout the camp. We were told that that same white van would arrive twice a week to give us a ride to a beach house outside of Pāʻia town. We could spend a couple of hours doing crafts and reading the Bible—and it was all for free.

On the first scheduled day, about five of us boarded the van and went to the beach house. I was very enthusiastic to have something to do. I put my long hair up in a French twist, which one of the teachers immediately commented on when I stepped into the van. She was surprised to see a French twist on a little Filipino youngster. She didn't know that I practiced a lot on hair by reading the monthly hair magazines that I thumbed through at Machida Drug Store.

At this summer school, young men and women from the Mainland came to Maui to do church work. Some of them had Southern accents and were very friendly, while others ignored us. Our instructor had a pleasant disposition and wanted to know all about us as well. She came with the van to pick us up one day, and they drove through our camp before heading for school. I wondered what she thought of us, but I was too polite to ask.

We were taught crafts such as pasting cotton balls onto colored construction paper that we turned into baskets. On another day, we sprinkled sand onto paper to create beach scenes. For homework, we each picked a passage from the Bible. Since I didn't have one at home, she lent me hers for the week. My passage wasn't as inspiring as others that were chosen. We also learned some Christian songs, but I forgot them after the summer. Our class liked her so much that we gave her a flower lei on the last day of class. She was touched by the thought and her dimples deepened as she smiled, trying to keep tears from filling her eyes.

Spirit of the Village

The Baptist interval filled the rest of summer. If their motive was to convert members, it didn't affect me. I continued to attend mass at Holy Rosary Church.

By the time August arrived, outside sounds that floated through the camp on invisible wings became more pronounced to me. Our dog Prince's chain rattled as he stepped into his doghouse, Tournahauler engines roared through the fields, and the roosters scratched their claws against slatted floors. There was also something different going on in another camp near ours.

The blaring noise over the loud speakers filled the night air with the "tonk-a-tonk, a-tonk-a-tonk" of a Japanese banjo and the accompanying beat of a *taiko* drum. The strange and eerie music landed on my pillow and crept into my ears, while the scent of mock orange perfumed the night. I called out to my father, "What is that?" My father said it was *obake* music. It was *Obon* season. These were the nights where Japanese honored the departed members of their families.

Aggie and her big sisters planned to go to the *Obon* dance. Since I was still very young, my father hesitantly permitted me to go, but after dark I walked with them to the Hongwanji Buddhist mission above our camp. The solo beam from our Eveready flashlight led our way. We took the dirt path between an open field and the Robia family's garden. *Gandule* bushes brushed up against our shoulders. Milkweeds and *kukū* poked our legs. We passed the *pūnāwai* and walked toward the mission across the street.

Like the start of a scene after the curtain rises, the congregation appeared against the blackness. People danced in a circle under colorful hanging lanterns and the white glittering stars of our Hawaiian skies. We stopped at the gate and propped ourselves up on the low wall made of smooth river rocks that surrounded the mission.

85

A Maui Memoir

We sat in the shadows because we were Filipino and did not want to bring attention to ourselves.

I saw Japanese women in colorful *kimono*—brilliant reds, blues and whites swirling in nature's wind over water, birds in flight, or flowers in full blossom. The brocaded *obi* shimmered with gold threads against silk kimonos and white *tabi*. They danced in large circles, sometimes three deep, moving in the same direction. The men danced too, wearing *hapi* coats—short hip length *kimono*-style jackets—loose but tied at the waist over their trousers. One or two men wore only white loincloths with their *hapi* coats, and walked on their *katas*, elevated wooden slippers. White narrow towels stretched across the back of their heads, both ends tied into a knot at the forehead. Their dance movements were simple, depicting farm work.

We caught on to the repeated steps and gestures, and we too danced from where we were on the stone wall, mimicking our Japanese neighbors, as if no one saw us.

Young men in white uniform danced with them, too. Ida said they were from Japan—cadets who sailed from their country to ours as part of their merchant marine training. This was a surprise to me. Japanese welcomed their sailors into their community, but American sailors weren't welcomed in ours. How strange.

When the music paused, the people dispersed throughout the courtyard, some for food and others to talk story. We didn't know whether we were welcome to eat, so we stayed put. But eventually, too excited to be still, we walked over to the temple.

Curious and reverent, I stepped into the *Hongwanji* temple to look inside. I expected to see people kneeling in pews and praying to statues of saints standing over them with sympathetic expressions. So I was in for a big surprise and gawked at the gold statue of

Spirit of the Village

a sitting Buddha dominating the altar ahead of us. His face was flat and without expression. His eyes were partly closed.

Scented smoke curled from hundreds of joss sticks standing in receptacles of sand. The smoke smelled like the scent of incense in our church during Benediction. In the temple, older Japanese people sat in chairs and meditated while the rest of the congregation danced through the night. I thought sitting was more civil than kneeling.

Outside, I walked past more paper lanterns that lit gravesites, revealing smooth headstones chiseled with Japanese calligraphy. Bowls of cooked rice, whole oranges, and other foods were placed near each one. Later I found out that these were offerings for the deceased for them to enjoy during their brief return on earth. My father was right. It was *obake* music. It was ghost music.

*

Although each group was a distant subculture, we intertwined daily with each other's ethnicity. For instance, Nashiwa Bakery was the meeting place for everyone, either to buy pastries, buy the daily papers, or wait for the school buses to bring us to Maui High School in Hāmākuapoko or to St. Anthony School in Wailuku. Adults of different ethnicity had their coffee and lunches there too, gossiping when they had the chance. Filipino men stood against the exterior wall facing the parking lot under the umbrella of a monkey pod tree.

These men, mostly single, were famous for holding "court" at Nashiwa's on Sunday mornings and making commentary about every person that passed in front of them, especially the women. It was either my aunt or *Manang* Minnie who nicknamed them the "Judges." My uncle was one of them. It was hopeless to avoid them as they were there as soon as the bakery opened at 5:30 a.m. On a few occasions, I made a point to rise early and attend First Mass. When I did, I had the chance to witness the Sunday morning "Judges."

These were moments when I wished I knew *Ilocano* or *Visayan* so I could understand what the men were saying. They were at their finest form when the parishioners who attended Low Mass flocked to the bakery an hour later for their Sunday pastries. Women hated to walk past them for fear of a whistle or a "psst" from a daring male, who enjoyed watching the women go by. Their comments were equally opinionated, whether it was a Filipino, Japanese, Portuguese or other female. I usually went to Second Mass, and by 10:00 a.m. most of the bakery's best pastries and the men were gone. But there was always a sugar or a glazed doughnut left. If I was lucky, I could get the last available newspaper, too. An hour before that, the "Judges" were headed for the cockfights.

Before society defined "cruelty to animals," cockfights were one of my favorite activities associated with my culture. It was something the adults did, unquestioningly. I could attend and watch without being chased away. I lived in the neighborhood where the regular weekend cockfights occurred.

From early morning, cars streamed into the village and parked along the green hibiscus hedges that framed the front yards. Men walked from their houses to the arena, two doors from where my aunt, uncle and cousin lived. The men wore clean shirts and trousers, and plastered down their shiny black hair with pomade. Their leather slippers were polished.

The arena buzzed with excited energy while the men waited for the event to begin. As men arrived, they gathered around in a circle, mostly forming groups under the shade of the mango trees, standing and talking in rapid guttural sounds of *Ilocano* and *Visayan*. An occasional English word popped up, "Steel blade," "F—!" Teenage boys stationed themselves at specific corners of the roads that led to our village. If the police approached, the boys whistled to one another, until one came running as fast as he could through the camp to alert the men. The crowd quickly hid the money and the blades. Everyone acted as if it was just a friendly afternoon of neighborhood visiting. If a raid occurred, two or three unmarked police cars sped to the spot in front of my aunt's. The police and detectives stepped out of their cars, grouped together, and walked toward the arena, cool and composed. One could tell they didn't belong, dressed in aloha shirts, dark glasses and all non-Filipinos. Since money or cocks were not in sight, they had no reason to arrest anyone. They walked around for a while, said hello to people they knew, and then returned to their cars. They slowly reversed and drove out of the village, not to return until the next time they needed to conduct a raid. Maui was too small to have enemies.

I knew when the fight was about to begin. Money exchanged hands. One man quickly walked around, collecting the green American bills from waving hands. I never knew how they kept tabs on every man who gave money. They spoke in Filipino and I had no idea what they were saying. Occasionally, one or two women stood among the men, but not often. I stayed behind the low unpainted picket fence separating Tata Mitchell's arena from Tata Anton's grassless front yard.

Each rooster was tethered to a long cotton twine, a braided leash with a six inch long fat nail at the other end, hammered into the hard dirt ground. The match was decided upon by weight and size of the roosters. The gamblers sized up the two roosters against each other, while others contemplated which cock was the strongest or the luckiest. Someone neutral tied the curved steel blades securely to each rooster's leg, usually my uncle. The bet was on which rooster would outlive the other.

When all the bettings subsided and the equally fit roosters matched, someone called out a signal—presumably a ready, set, go! The owners tossed their birds into the barren ring and watched the action. The two roosters eyed each other, stepping cautiously and bantering in a circle for a minute or so before one attempted an attack on the other. I didn't know what compelled these roosters to fight, but soon they were at each other, flying through the air, golden neck feathers standing on end, silver blades glistening and smeared with fresh red blood.

I watched my uncle with delight when it was his rooster in the ring. He hopped on one leg, then the other, shouting with enthusiasm, running around the arena. His body jerked from left to right, while he watched his rooster out-maneuver the other. "Come on!" "You lose, Boy!" "*Make* o'ready!" His Hawaiian Creole interspersed with the Filipino phrases, *"Aiyee, Apo!" "Ti uki ni nam!"*

I loved the excitement that burst from the men as they cheered if they won and razzed each other if they lost. After the cockfights were over, I imagined that most of them, especially the single men, returned to sparse rooms and resumed their humdrum lives.

In our camp, most of the *single men* that came to Hawai'i for a better life left their families in the Philippines. Some were unmarried until they retired, returning to their homeland rich by PI standards. Others wrote letters to young women back in the Philippines, wooing them with photos of their younger selves, only to shock their mail order wives when they stepped on the tarmac at the Kahului Airport. In one incident, the old man approached his young bride-to-be while she looked beyond him searching for the young man she fell in love with in the photo. Her smile and hope dropped when he introduced himself as her new husband. She couldn't turn and walk back into the plane and go home. She was here for good now.

I wondered why these arrangements occurred so often in our culture. When they did, we children made fun of the couple, although some of them had good relationships and their marriages worked out. Factors that were unknown to me then became apparent when I was older. Later I realized that it fulfilled a woman's chance for the "American Dream." (In 2003 I speculated that these mail-order marriages might have filled the void of the reduced Filipino male population during World War II.)

I recognized the *single men* in our camp by face but hardly knew any of them by their full name.

There was Clemente, our village drunk, staggering home after a day of drinking, his face red with whiskey, but smiling at me with a semi-toothless grin. The boys gave him a nickname, Clemente Fu-lo-ba-se (Clemente full of whiskey). He lived in my Uncle Pimio's barracks

91

until someone beat him up. After that, he disappeared from the camp. I recognized some *single men* by their cars, and we had nicknames for them too—like "Cadillac," pronounced *Cah-dee-lock*, accent on the last syllable. He earned his nickname from the car he owned.

Others that we did not nickname were respected by the younger set because they weren't flamboyant or had "reputations." One such man was *Tata* Mitchell. His front yard was the dirt floor arena for the camp's cockfights. Cockfights occurred seasonally on Sundays, after the roosters molted and their new shiny feathers covered their bodies again with alluring colors of red, yellow, black and gold.

Following his day shift in the fields, *Tata* Mitchell swept the arena clean of mango leaves that fell from the hanging branches of his old fruit trees. Sometimes I'd creep up behind him and shout, "Boo!" like he did to us, whenever he saw us playing in the road in front of his house. *Tata* Mitchell lived alone, but his yard was big enough to host activities—cockfights, as well as *Hanafuda* and *Payut*, card games that the men, and some women, played for small wagers.

After Sunday cockfights, *Tata* Mitchell's front yard emptied again, left like a set waiting for the next act. In the evenings, the small card games continued at the tall legged tables that were permanently stationed there. People stood at these tables to play, under a bare light bulb suspended from an extension cord, braided through the limbs of a mango tree.

In my box of old photos, there is a photo of Tata Mitchell at his retirement farewell in the sugar cane fields in the '60s. The photo included my father and the rest of the crew, made up of other Filipinos and two Portuguese luna. He worked for the plantation for most of his adult life. For his retirement gift, the luna presented *Tata* Mitchell with a plastic clock radio.

I eventually lost contact with *Tata* Mitchell. I believe he moved in with a family whose father originally came from the same province in the Philippines as *Tata* Mitchell. His front yard, however, was one of the places I roamed when I was bored and looking for some sort of activity. The memories of those many cockfights are still vivid to me.

By 2:00 p.m. on a Sunday afternoon, the fights diminished, the crowd dispersed, and the winner brought the presumably dead rooster home for the evening's dinner.

"Honeey! I win." My uncle shouted from the front steps of their porch. Of course my Auntie Nora already knew that since I ran to her immediately after the fight was over to tell her that Uncle's rooster had won. With her weekly ironing completed by this time, she was ready to clean and stew Sunday dinner.

She put a tall soup pot of water to boil on the gas stove. My aunt took hold of the rooster's neck while Andy and I grasped its wings to avoid its unscheduled flight through the kitchen. Although supposedly dead, the bird gave quite a struggle when my aunt deftly slit its throat with her kitchen knife. My cousin and I held its wings as tight as our little hands could as she placed a small dish of raw rice kernels under its bleeding neck to catch the fresh blood. When all of its blood dripped over the rice kernels, she put it in the refrigerator.

The bird's body jerked and twitched as its eyelids closed, giving up its last ounce of life to us. The hot water from the pot was then quickly poured over its entire body to loosen its feathers without parboiling the bird. It was our chore to pluck all the feathers off. The smell of bird

93

and feathers rose into my nostrils as the hot water steamed from the enamel sink. My finger tips burned from the heat.

After the bird was plucked naked, my aunt cleaned it by pulling its innards out. Carefully keeping the intestines intact, she rinsed the *battikuleng* by slitting it and turning it inside out to empty out the coarse grain and small pebbles that the rooster had pecked on previously. She placed this in the refrigerator also until it was time to add it to the soup. The rest of the innards were discarded.

She then rubbed the inside and outside of the carcass with salt and rinsed it well, usually with the first rinse water from the evening's pot of rice. This was used to eliminate any odor from the carcass. After patting it dry, she passed it over the open flame on the gas stove to singe any small feathers that we missed. She made sure every feather was burned off before she cut the body into pieces. She started with separating the carcass at the joints, then chopped through the bone into smaller chunks, and lastly rubbed the pieces with salt to clean any impurities from the meat. After rinsing the salt off, she sautéed the pieces with fresh ginger in the soup pot and covered it with cold water. She dropped the *battikuleng* in too. All during this time, I stood near her and watched every move she made. I felt like a movie camera taping everything.

To break down the toughness of the fighting bird, the soup simmered for at least three to four hours. Every once in awhile, she lifted the cover and skimmed off the top of the soup. While we waited, my aunt recruited me to pick the vegetables with her that she would later add to the soup. Our vegetables were the leaves either from the *paria* vines or *marunggay* trees.

Spirit of the Village

One afternoon, we squatted side by side in *Tata* Anton's *paria* (bittermelon) patch. His *banyo* shaded half of the patch while the other side was open to the full sun. We started at the cool side first and worked our way through the patch as the sun settled in the distance, giving us some comfort as we worked. She showed me how to pinch the tender shoots off the vine first with my right hand and then hold the shoots with my left. We also picked the matured leaves whem the shoots were not plentiful. The softer, tender leaves were not as bitter as the older and tougher ones. This was a time to think. I figured she probably thought of what she needed to do for the rest of the evening to prepare dinner, clean up and then sort out the lunches for the next work day. I daydreamed about the small bugs that crawled under the vines and scurried away when my fingers approached their hiding places. My thoughts were to myself. Without paying attention, I could methodically do anything once I knew the procedure. For me, these were moments when I didn't have to think about homework, housework or my mother. I was doing something useful and I wasn't accused of being idle.

If Auntie chose *marunggay* leaves instead of the *paria*, she'd pick a handful of the fern-like branches and place them on her dining table in the kitchen. We sat around the table and stripped the clover-shaped leaves from the stems into her aluminum colander. It took time to gather and clean these vegetables, but they are fortified with vitamin C and iron. It didn't matter which vegetables we used for this soup, as they both melted down to almost nothing if we didn't pick enough.

When the soup was about done, she slipped the liver and blood with raw rice into the soup. It took another 15 minutes to cook. She added salt and *patis* for flavoring and laid the vegetables on top to steam. This chicken soup was called, *biagan*, named after the cock fights.

After dinner, the kitchen was cleaned up—dishes washed, dried and put away. The floor was completely swept and mopped, and the rice for next morning's *kau kau tin* soaked in the rice pot.

After her bath, my aunt sat near the floor lamp so that the light cast on her crocheting. She positioned her graceful fingers in mid air in front of her, bending her elbow comfortably at waist height, working the fingers to slacken or tighten the thread, and maneuvering a steel hook, size 2, with the fingers of her right hand. The single cotton thread wound around her ring finger once and then over her forefinger which also held the thread in place with her thumb. The thread trailed from a ball hidden in a make-shift basket made from a brown paper grocery sack. The sack was folded over at its opening to form a collar that stiffened and kept itself from collapsing. When I looked into the sack, I saw many roses—made of thread that were single, double and triple crocheted. These blossoms were weavings from her evening ritual that when gathered, formed an entirely intricate handmade bedspread.

While she tended to her crocheting, my uncle prepared his cockfighting paraphernalia, such as waxing yards of cotton string and sharpening the blades. He called them his "knives." The roosters wore these on one leg during the fight.

Regardless of the violent killing these birds were subjected to, the diligent care I saw my uncle put into his beloved pastime was special.

For the spurs, he spent hours stretching out his right arm, pulling yards of string through a block of bees wax he held in his left palm, his mind in meditation. When he slid each blade out of its sheath cut into a specially made wooden box, I saw pride in his eyes as he lifted each one to the light to make sure it was razor sharp. He smiled when I asked him questions about the blade he held in his hand, as he admired the sharpness and brilliance of the weapon, assuring a quick as lightning kill.

I spent a lot of time at my aunt's house after my mom left. My auntie was shorter than my mother and squarer in shape. She didn't have a figure like her sister, but she had a pretty face like my mother, Rose. She enjoyed dressing up for church or when they went "night-clubbing." The two sisters spent a lot of time on their makeup. Some nights when my mother was still with us, they dressed together in front of my auntie's mirror, matching jewelry, and powdering their faces as their husbands commented on their tardiness. I watched and admired them as they prettied up for the evening. When they were ready, my aunt's high stiletto heels accentuated her short stride as she scurried next to my tall uncle to keep up with his long ones.

My uncle was very particular about the way he dressed. When they went out, he wore the best silk shirts my aunt bought for him from Peggy and Johnny's. The shirts were beautiful printed aloha shirts with cranes, flowers or waves that were vibrant with color but never gaudy. Like my father, he washed and polished their 1957 Oldsmobile every weekend before they went out. Their car was identical to ours. During the week, they stayed home and sat in front of the television or practiced their dance steps.

They loved to dance. At night, Andy and I were their audience as they cha-cha-chaed in their living room to Xavier Cugat LP's. During the day, alone in my own living room, I repeated the steps that they practiced the night before. I was a pretty good dancer if all I had to do was dance alone. In the late 1980's when he celebrated his 70th birthday, I asked my Uncle for a dance. It took all that time for me to find the courage to ask him.

My uncle came home from the fields, dirty from hat to shoes. I stayed out of his way because his mood wasn't always pleasant. One afternoon, as he laid his *kau kau tin* down on the steps, he looked up at me through the screen door and growled, "You get op' d' pone. All da time you on d' pone." My cousin was watching television. I didn't understand why it was all right for him to be watching TV and it wasn't all right for me to be speaking to a friend on the telephone. Disgusted, I hung up the phone and went home. But he mellowed out after he bathed, put on a fresh white t-shirt and pants, and headed to his chicken yard in the back. The back was cooled by a spreading mango tree that shaded the chicken coops and the back lawn. While the sun settled into the west, the trade winds soothed my uncle after a day in the hot and dusty sugar cane fields. His heart and soul was in his livestock. My uncle's fighters were raised by his hands only. He spoke to them, pet them and treated them well. He raised them from hatching eggs to yellow chicks, to adult fighters. He built a wooden incubator for the young chicks, where they snuggled and slept together under a warm bulb. At night, I would lift the canvas flap that covered their screen window and observed them as they chirped, drank water and snuggled up close to the bulb for warmth. I smelled the aroma of fresh ground corn and grain. It was nice. After their feathers grew in, though, the only contact I had was hearing the scratching of their feet against the floor slats of their individual coops. Their area was swept every afternoon to prevent flies and other bugs from living in the manure that dropped to the ground between the slats of their coops.

It was hard to tell which rooster was the best. Every afternoon, Uncle Aning tethered one or two roosters by tying one leg of a rooster with a cotton leash. The leash was connected to a long nail that he pounded into the ground. That way the roosters exercised without running away. They were quite beautiful and bold in their new feathers—scarlet, golden and rust against dark blue feathers that were deep enough to be black. Their blood red combs stood upright over their intense eyes and yellow beaks. My uncle allowed me to carry one once, which I discovered to be a mass of hard muscle, unlike the little soft chick it once was.

The existence of fighting roosters was part of our lifestyle in Orpheum Village. I'd prefer a bowl or two of my auntie's *biagan* soup over any dish today. (When animal rightists protested about cockfighting later in the '60s, I had difficulty admitting that cockfights were cruel.)

From their backyard, I could see my father at our kitchen sink, washing his *kau kau tin* after he finished his shift. Our house was visible behind the hibiscus hedges that bordered my maternal grandfather's house and my aunt's. I knew my father was there whenever I needed him. He did not talk much, but his presence was always comforting to me, especially during the times when I was ill. He would reluctantly give up a day or two of work because he would not get paid. My father raised his share of fighting cocks too, but the hobby did not last long. After my mom left, his hobby slowly dwindled. It was partly due to the unpaid bills that accumulated while she was still home. She was secretly saving their money and neglecting the bills. Companies garnisheed his paycheck. His last birds were slaughtered for our dinners. My mother's private plans prevented him from having a life without financial stress. I was still attending private school when we had to buy a new washer. I brought the monthly payment of $5.00 over to Pā'ia Mercantile to pay it off. The clerk always asked how my father was doing. It seemed like all of Pā'ia knew that my father struggled, except me. I was shielded from a lot of things.

Nevertheless, we always had food on the table. He did all the cooking after he returned from work. If he worked the night shift, sausages or dried *aku* were stocked in the refrigerator for me to heat up. On those lonely afternoons after school, I had every intention to doing my homework. But as soon as I got into the house, I watched television or ate whatever snacks were in the refrigerator. I was bored. The homework didn't get done until later in the evening. I procrastinated and let other things get in the way. One nice thing, though, was that I made friends with the neighbors I couldn't play with before, when my mother chose my playmates. Quickly, I became friends with Beverly.

Part of our pastime was preparing every concoction known to our young minds to enhance the fruits that grew abundantly around us. Green guavas, half-ripe mangoes, wild purple plums, green acerola cherries, all went into dipping sauces of shoyu, vinegar, and sugar. These fruits were plentiful in Beverly's yard, and if we couldn't find them there, we'd get them from someone else's yard. We knew where every fruit tree existed in the camp. We dipped our sliced green mangos into *bagoong*. The salt counteracted the sourness of the unripe mango. Another neighbor, Debbie, found a jicama growing wild in the fields behind our neighborhood, between the *pūnāwai* and the *Hongwanji* Mission. She recognized the structure of the plant, dug up the dirt around it and produced a large white root. After dusting it off, she immediately bit into it and offered me some. With some hesitation, I tried it. It was amazingly sweet and crunchy.

But I liked sweet juices more than I craved green mangos and *bagoong*, and the *liliko'i* juice that Ida made was my favorite. She looked at the *liliko'i* sitting on the window sill in their kitchen. They were puckered up and looked like something ready for the trash bin. The fruit grew wild over their pig pens in Kaheka. She chose several of them and cut the fruit in half. Golden rich pulp immediately oozed out along with black round seeds. She placed them into the middle of a piece of cloth and twisted the cloth tightly as she squeezed juice from the pulp and seeds with her one palm, letting the liquid drip into a glass. The cloth was now the color of pure yellow sunlight. A generous amount of sugar and more water was added to the delicious juice packed with vitamin C.

It was that way at all the houses I visited in the camp. There was always something good and different available to eat at any of my neighbors' homes. I was never turned away. Our own offering came from the old avocado tree that grew in our yard, taller than our house. It produced so many avocados one year that we were able to supply the neighborhood and then send a box loaded with the fruit to cousins Benny and Anita on Oʻahu. *Tata* Poro climbed the limbs high above our heads and dropped avocados down below to his son who caught them and loaded them into a burlap bag. He filled the bag many times; sometimes it was hard to see where *Tata* Poro stood balancing on a branch high in the tree.

With the summer months passing and the fruit disappearing, my independence ballooned.

Being alone at night while my father worked the

night shift was something I forced myself to do. I preferred to stay home.

Activity after dark in Pā'ia did not only mean coming home from the fields after a night's shift or driving home on the lonely highway from the canneries. For me, it also meant meeting apparitions. One night, I walked to my aunt's. It was still early in the evening, about 8:30 p.m. I made the left turn on to my aunt's road, approaching my grandfather's dark house on the corner. I could see her yellow porch light on. It would not take long for me to get there, as I passed my grandfather's hibiscus hedges, coconut tree, and his lawn under the sprawling monkey pod tree. I looked toward my grandpa's Samoan coconut tree and caught a glimpse of a silhouette standing next it. The figure was dark, but I also saw an outline of a hat on the person's head. It was the type of hat the men wore in the '40s. I stared at the figure as I walked past it. It didn't make a sound and it didn't move. But I ran.

My aunt heard my hurried heavy footsteps on her porch and came to the screened door. She wrapped her bathrobe over her torso. "Why you come so late?" she asked. I didn't think it was late. "I did my homework first, Auntie," I answered. "Come and do your homework here next time." she replied. She unlatched the screen door to let me in. "No let the mosquitoes in!" she grumbled. Above my head, geckos flocked to the yellow light bulb that hung from the porch's ceiling. "Auntie, there's someone standing over there." I pointed toward the coconut tree. "Whea?" She shuffled to the edge of the porch and looked cautiously into the black night. She hushed me into the house. "No mo' no body," she said, and that was that. I stepped lightly through the kitchen and into Andy's room in order to get to the middle room. His breathing was steady and he was already in deep sleep. In the next room, I crawled into the bed next to my older female cousin from the P.I.

Whether or not that figure was real, I always thought it was the appearance of my Uncle Eusebio who wore that sort of hat when he was alive.

Weeks passed and I demanded that my father come for me after his night shift, regardless of how late it was. So for the next few nights, he agreed and knocked on the wooden wall of the bedroom to signal me. I stumbled out of the bed and walked home with him shortly before midnight. We must have interrupted everyone's sleep in the household because he stopped doing that after a while, and I became very upset.

By age 10, I decided that I didn't have to go to my aunt's house anymore. I stayed home alone one night and locked the front door. Everyone in the neighborhood knew each other and there was no one to be afraid of. I preferred the comfort of the surroundings of my own house and my familiar bedroom. I had moved into my mother's old room. The space was mine and I liked the freedom. The only sounds in the night were the hissing of the Pā'ia Mill letting off its steam, and the tournahaulers rumbling in the fields. Our dog, Prince, only barked if a toad or stray cat crossed our driveway. Other than that, he didn't bark much. He knew every scent of every person that passed our yard and house. There were no threats.

From then on, when my father worked nights, all the lights in the house remained on until I was ready for bed. Even then, I kept my ears tuned for any kind of noises outside that I wasn't familiar with. I usually stayed up very late, keeping the television on or playing my 45 rpm records for company.

In time, I befriended another girl up the road from me who had lost her mother also, but in childbirth. Flora had two brothers and a sister. Her father played cards with his friends most evenings, so Flora and I spent a lot of time together.

One night, she was visiting at my house. Being young teens, it wasn't unusual for us to accompany each other while we took our baths. She sat on the raised wooden toilet that faced the shower and the four-paned window above our concrete sink. The flat round shower head sprayed water over my head directly onto the concrete floor. Rafters were exposed under the corrugated tin roof. Beyond the window, a narrow space overgrown with weeds separated the *banyo* and the small shed that stored boxes of personal items and garden tools. As we gossiped and giggled, Flora suddenly stopped talking and stared out the window above the sink.

"Jackie, what's that?" she whispered. "What?" I said and covered my flat chest. I watched her as she jumped down from the toilet and to the window. We heard a rustling through the weeds and Flora screamed, "Somebody stay outside!"

I yelled and quickly crouched behind the sink. She shouted *"HEY!"* to the emptiness outside as she jumped up and down with anxiety. In a flash, she scrambled to the door, unlatched it and ran outside. I put my clothes over my wet body. "Flora?" I whispered. No answer. "Flora?" Still no reply. Eventually, she returned to the *banyo* with a bewildered look on her face. "Jackie, you better put a curtain on the window." She took a deep breath and said cautiously, "Somebody was smoking a cigarette and watching you." Flora had seen a red glow brighten to an orange point each time the peeping Tom inhaled. I was glad that Flora was there or else I wouldn't have known I was being watched. After that, I took my showers before dark or when my neighbors took theirs.

Spirit of the Village

Slowly, I lost the good habits that my mother instilled in me. I now talked on the phone for hours, stayed up late watching television, and ate whenever I desired. My school work was incomplete and the house turned into a dust bin.

My father and aunt expected me to clean the house now that my mother was gone. I gave myself a crash course in housekeeping. Sometimes I mopped the portion of the floor just next to the entry at the verandah and the living room so my father would think I cleaned the house. He was not as ignorant as I suspected. He checked the opposite corners of the room, behind the television and sofa, and saw the brown Pāʻia dust mount until the next spurt of energy overcame me. The dust collected on the opened windowsills, on the running board of the walls, on the floor boards, in the curtains and on the white Venetian blinds. I acquired an allergy to dust. I was rebelling but didn't know why.

The rest of the family experienced their own set of emotions about my mother's absence, but they showed no signs of obvious distress. I couldn't tell when someone was upset until they screamed at me to "Shut up" or to "Go away." That was how the family reacted to my mother's absence. We weren't educated to realize that circumstances such as my mother's absence made a difference to us. We weren't taught to express our feelings. So when these feelings affected me, I couldn't explain them. My personality changed and I kept my thoughts to myself, afraid to voice them. From my outward appearance, I gathered that my aunt thought I was lazy or stupid—most of the time, both.

On the good side, I made more friends now that my mother was not around to censor my acquaintances. I spent a lot of time with Fely, too. She had four handsome brothers, and her father was also a great cook who catered some of the large parties we had in the camp.

One evening when I spent the night with her, I noticed her father propped against his pillows in bed, reading *The Honolulu Advertiser* under a 60 watt light bulb hanging from the ceiling. The family television's volume was high in the living room, but he was engrossed in his reading. I was surprised because it was seldom that I saw adults in my camp reading a paper or a book. Men were either going to or coming home from work. The women were either in church or doing household chores. My aunt read her *True Confession* magazines or the Sunday paper. I thought only school children had to read books. But Mr. Leoncio Soliven was an avid reader. He was interested in politics, too. He read about everything pertaining to the President of the Philippines who was killed in an airplane crash that year, and the Catholic candidate who was about to become the President of the United States. I thought the candidate for president was handsome and I hoped he would win. While walking to church one day, Fely said, "My father said we going get war if we get one Democrat for president." That didn't cheer me up at all.

My father also read occasionally. He read the first letter from my mother since she had left. He read it aloud to me before school. We sat in our 1957 blue and white Oldsmobile in the parking lot of the church, and he read the letter carefully, maybe skipping parts that weren't meant for me. Tears rose in my eyelids. I clung to every word he read. She was not coming home. When the school bell rang, I asked him if I could go home instead. I did not want to go to classes that day.

Another time, a salesman came to our village and sold books, door to door, written in Filipino. My father bought one and he read it every afternoon after he finished work. One afternoon, I walked into the veranda where he sat on the pune'e reading that book. His elbows rested on his thighs with his arms extended to balance the book in his palms. I saw tears roll down his cheeks as he read the book about Dr. Jose Rizal, National Hero of the Philippines.

My father kept his P.I. Citizenship until he died. Every January, I picked up a green card for him to fill in and sign, and then return to the post office. His dream was to return to his homeland when he retired. He did that later in his life, but he always came home—to Maui.

He also read my left palm one day. He didn't say that I would be traveling to far off places as an adult. But as it was, he only acknowledged my future with a slap on the palm and a disgruntled, "Hmf." He didn't seem happy with what he saw.

At the close of our eighth grade year at Holy Rosary School in 1962, we were notified that we were the last class to graduate. Most of the families had moved out of Pā'ia already and there weren't enough students to keep the school open. My plans were to start my freshman year at St. Anthony Girls School after the summer. That juxtaposed with the news that my mother, Rose, was coming home to visit. She had not been back since 1959 and she was returning in time for my graduation. I hadn't seen or spoken to her in three years. I felt really excited and my imagination ran wild. I imagined that all good things would happen when she came home. A new white dress was tailored for my graduation, I had a new perm, and I would see my mother again.

The graduation ceremony was solemn and held in Holy Rosary Church. It reminded me of my first communion, when we sat in the front and center pews, the girls in white dresses, veils, and patent leather flats,

107

like little brides; and the boys in white long sleeve shirts, black ties, trousers and shoes. For this occasion, the veils were eliminated but the dresses were pretty similar. Our parents and relatives sat behind us. At my first communion—I had turned around to see where my mother was sitting, but she wasn't in the pew where I saw her previously. I didn't see her anywhere. At my graduation, I dared not look around for my mother. My father was sitting somewhere in church, I had hoped.

After the ceremony, we marched in file toward the exit. Our eighth grade teacher stood between the two angel statues that held the holy water. She hugged each one of us as we passed, and made us promise that we'd be successful from then on. It was a long time since I had been hugged and I felt very awkward.

Success was a big concept, but I nodded in agreement. I didn't know what success meant. As far as success was concerned, I thought it was for other people and not for me.

I walked outside to the parking lot, hesitant but hopeful. I saw my father in the car waiting. When I asked him where my mother was, he said she and my aunt left earlier. He was quiet that day. He asked me what I wanted to do next. I asked, "Can we take pictures?" He consented and drove to Nagamine Studio on Baldwin Avenue. Mr. Nagamine was kind and urged me to smile, but I didn't feel like it. By the looks of my graduation photo, I wasn't overjoyed. I thought the sleeves of my dress were too long. My hair was too curly after a tightly made permanent. My teeth grew out with spaces between them. I wasn't the beauty princess I wanted to be. Although my mother was home for the summer and high school was to begin, my graduation day did not meet my expecations.

Spirit of the Village

After the photo session, my father drove us home. I excused myself and walked over to my aunt's. She and my mom were at the kitchen table gossiping just like in old times. They were best friends after all. They discussed how Andy and I had grown and how we looked. My mother smiled at me and said, "You know Jackie, you're pretty, but you're dark."

By this time, I knew I felt sad but I didn't know why. I didn't speak to anyone about my feelings and no one asked me about them either. I missed my mother so much.

But I wasn't the only one that was unhappy and needed an outlet, it seemed. Regular fist fights were scheduled between girls from Pā'ia School, just because one looked sideways at the other. Days before the fight, a handwritten note, passed on from one hand to the other, would reach across the street from Pā'ia School to ours. We were told who was challenging whom. Immediately after our school bells rang, handfuls of students congregated under the monkey pod tree next to the sugarcane fields before Green and Nashiwa Camps. Most of the time, the fights were between two rivals from the public school. During one of the bouts, a girl cried not from the punches that were delivered, but from her skirt lifted by her opponent to expose her underwear. I felt it was humiliating for the girl left lying on the ground. I watched in the sidelines like the others. This was the way we knew how to solve matters. I didn't realize that it was depression that caused our gloom.

Often, my walk home after school was spent deliberating how I could win a fist fight in the event I was ever picked on. Anger built up inside of me and the only way to release it was to create imaginary fights with female bullies. Luckily, I was never involved in a physical confrontation. My 65 pound frame could never have endured the punishment from punches.

I was brought up to think that my brown skin was inferior compared to white skin. Not just by my family but by remarks that I overheard, but said without intended harm. Remarks like "Those damn Filipinos," "Lazy *Kanaka*" or "They're *Portagee*, that's why," were planted in my mind. I was inclined to believe that there was something else attached to them. *Haoles* seemed to be treated better than we were. They lived in bigger houses and had the better jobs. They told my parents what to do. I felt insignificant. I knew the feeling of being second best. Besides, my mother wasn't around anymore to lift my spirits, to dress me in pretty clothes, and to tell me that I was smart. If that wasn't enough to make me insecure about my appearance, my feelings were equally hurt when my mother's new husband arrived to join her. This tall, muscular, blond, blue-eyed Dutchman worked as a film extra in Hollywood. I was introduced to him as her niece. She didn't want him to know about her past and me. I kept my disappointment and feelings of rejection inside again by not mentioning them to anyone.

I think that she and her husband made tongues wag and eyes pop. To me, they acted and dressed differently from the community I belonged to. He pedaled seven miles down to Baldwin Park from Orpheum Camp everyday, and pedaled back wearing only his swimming briefs. This was a unique sight, especially since the majority of Pā'ia's population was short, Asian and dressed modestly. Sometimes she, in her skimpy bikini, sat on the bicycle handles as he pedaled to their destinations.

Regardless, my spirit lifted and my whole body felt lighter every time I was near her. That deep void in my heart disappeared.

Spirit of the Village

I returned daily to my aunt's at dinner time, where we dined on fresh fish caught by local divers or whatever my aunt decided to serve that night. My mother and her husband maintained their diet of raisins, yogurt and nuts. They were health food addicts from Venice, California. I never saw two people eat so much lettuce in those days.

My father remained in the background. The entire neighborhood seemed quiet during that month that they visited. Everyone kept to themselves, and no one came to my aunt's to visit. My mother wanted to see our house once again and I acted as the "go-between." I asked my father and he permitted it. During one of his night shifts, she and I walked to the house and sat in the living room for a few minutes. My father and I left everything about the same as when she left, except it was not as spotless as when she did the housekeeping.

We sat in the living room for a while, she sitting on the sofa where she used to write. I don't know what thoughts sped through her mind since she didn't share them with me. I hoped maybe she would stay. Eventually, she suggested that we walk back to Auntie's house. "Are you coming home?" I asked. She shook her head.

From then on, my hopes of her coming back to us dissipated with each passing day. I lost interest, and the longing I had for her. I stayed away from her and sought my playmates.

One morning I walked down to Auntie's house; my mother stood in the front yard watering the ti plants and orchids. She shouted out loud when she saw me, "Where have you been? You know that I am here, but you don't come around!" I felt odd. I thought I wasn't welcomed especially when her husband was nearby. She ignored me, or scolded me when I called her "Mommy." So what was she complaining about? I wanted to tell her, but I was too timid to say how I felt. I really wanted to say, *"You not coming home, das why!"* We won't be living as a family again. I wanted everything to be the same as it was before. Would that explain all the hurt I felt inside?

Then summer ended. Her husband had already left and now it was her turn to leave.

The Kahului Airport was a two room terminal with a separate snack shop. Two airline counters stood opposite each other in the main room. In the next room, doors lined up as gates between large windows, backless benches made a middle row and another row against the concrete wall. We stood in the middle of the room when her flight was announced over the PA system. She hugged me close to her and I could not let go of her. Her lavender shift was damp where my eyes touched the fabric at her hip. She was the last one to pass the gate after I reluctantly let go.

We corresponded after that. I ranted in one of my letters. I preached that she was a sinner because she didn't go to church anymore. I was frustrated. I was only 12 years old. What did I know?

The rest of the summer was hot and boring. My clothes started to fit differently and my body changed from thin to plump. My neighbor, Fely, and I were tomboys but growing into young women.

If I wasn't at home, I was at Fely's house or climbing trees with her. Her older brothers were either in the front yard working on their hot rods or working in the pineapple cannery or fields. She and I roamed the neighborhood and explored various discreet paths and discovered other backyards. A favorite hideaway was in a young mango tree that grew between *Tata* Anton and my aunt's backyard, across the road from Fely's driveway. A small gate made from chicken wire and two by four's locked with a latch divided the backyards from the road.

But anyone could unlock it and pass through. Fely and I unlocked the gate and climbed up the mango tree. We pulled ourselves up the trunk holding on to a low branch. We put our feet on the roof of the chicken coops, and then found a sturdy branch that felt comfortable to sit on. The height gave us a view of the rooftops, the houses up and down the road, and the freedom to dream of faraway places.

The trade winds cooled our young bodies in the mid-afternoon's summer heat. Mangoes too small to eat hung in clumps like big grapes all around us. Soon, we heard the gate unlatch and the crunch of dry leaves. Under us, a *single man* walked through the gate and latched it behind him. Quietly, Fely pulled a small mango off its branch and dropped it on the man's head. He brushed the top of his head without looking up and continued on. She did it again, this time we both giggled and the man looked up into the tree. *"Ti uki ni nam,"* he swore and walked on.

Sometimes Fely brought her small transistor radio up into the tree with us. We listened to KPOI Radio with Steve Nicolet or Tom Moffatt, our favorite disc jockeys. Motown music played between The Young Rascals, Teddy Randazzo, Connie Francis, Ray Peterson, and Wayne Newton—just names that come to mind. We sat in the tree for hours or until her mother called out for us to walk with her down to the Post Office, across the street from the Pā'ia Mill, more than a mile from where we lived.

I admired Fely. She had smooth shiny skin like creamed coffee, a long nose and gracefully bowed lips. She was also "thin as a rail," as her mother used to say. The clothes that her mother, *Manang* Minnie, ordered for her from the Alden's Catalog always fit her. Unlike my clothes that my aunt ordered—mine were always too big. My aunt had this philosophy: in time I'd grow into my clothes. Well, it took about five years before I could fit into the clothes she ordered for me.

Manang Minnie rejoiced when she received her first Sears Catalog in the mail. We didn't have a Sears store on Maui then, but this catalog gave her a wider selection to choose from. I hurried home and asked my father to subscribe to a Sears Catalog too, although we already had the Aldens.

One afternoon, I walked into their living room to find *Manang* Minnie kneeling on her floor, cutting some pieces of tissue paper that was pinned to material. General Hospital entertained her from their TV set. I asked her what she was doing. She continued to cut the pieces while she explained, "This is the facing for the neck. This one is for the sleeve." Her portable sewing machine was already on the coffee table of their mahogany set. A red spool of thread rested on the spindle. "I teach you how to sew if you like. Mo' cheap if you sew your own clothes," she advised me.

That summer I sewed my first few projects on her sewing machine. Fely and I were on a roll, and we competed for time on the sewing machine. *Manang* Minnie suggested that I ask my dad if he would buy a sewing machine for me, too. He eventually did.

I heard about a sewing class given at the Hongwanji Mission by Mrs. Okuda, I never knew her first name. She willingly accepted us into her class. Another friend and I were the only Filipinos in a class of Japanese girls. Sometimes the girls looked up at us and smiled condescendingly, nodding their heads as if approving. They kept to themselves, but it didn't matter. My friend and I giggled a lot between stitches, and I was learning something constructive. I also enjoyed it. Mrs. Okuda taught us how to draft patterns with a numbering method and a special curved ruler. We came into class with ideas or images cut from magazines. She guided each of us through the drafting process.

I made a double breasted sleeveless shift with a Peter Pan collar and two rows of buttons down the front made from soft Hunter's Green corduroy fabric. It needed lots of pattern pieces but with Mrs. Okuda's help, it was easy. I also drafted a pattern for a men's shirt which I used various times to sew shirts for my father. He was proud of the first shirt that I sewed for him, and I was secretly pleased that he wore it so often. Mrs. Okuda's training was valuable information that, unfortunately, I eventually forgot. But I continued to sew most of my own clothes throughout high school with patterns from *Simplicity* or *McCalls*.

My way of keeping up with the recent fashion in clothing and hair was by reading those monthly magazines that were displayed on the racks at Machida Drugs in Lower Pā'ia. I waited for the newest issues of *Teen* magazine with the photos of *American Bandstand* regulars and news of Hollywood Stars like Sandra Dee and Bobby Darin. I looked at hair magazines to learn about the latest hairdos. The wedge look was popular that year, so I practiced on mine and my playmate, Beverly's hair. I thought it turned out all right.

The *American Bandstand* show had a big influence on my teen years, especially the music and the dance steps. I bought every 45 rpm record that the Supremes made. At four o'clock each Thursday, I taught myself the "Mash Potatoes," the "Continental," and the "Pony" by watching the couples dancing in front of the cameras. It was a good thing that I was usually alone because there was only enough room for one. I moved the coffee table aside to have sufficient room to dance my afternoon away. I also did not miss a local broadcast on

Oʻahu that provided an afternoon program similar to *American Bandstand*. My favorite dancer was Yvonne Elliman, long before she became a singing star. She was easy to spot by her Maryknoll High School uniform.

When these shows weren't on, I danced to Martha and the Vandellas, the Chiffons, Roy Orbison and other vocalists whose recordings gave me an escape from my life in the camp. I sang along with the vocalists and exercised my vocal chords. My hi-fi phonograph was a vehicle for dreaming.

Then summer vacation ended and it was time to attend high school. Before classes started in September, my aunt and I went to the bookstore on the St. Anthony Girls School campus in Wailuku to purchase my books and uniform. There were so many books to acquire. Freshman classes required texts and workbooks for Algebra, Religion, Latin, World History and Literature. We bought white collared blouses with short sleeves, and blue a-lined skirts with sleeveless boleros. My aunt, with her concern for money, insisted I buy a size larger, so I wouldn't have to buy another set the following year. She hemmed the skirt up but I "swam" in the blouse and bolero. I bought the matching white socks with black and white oxfords at Roland's Shoe Store in Kahului. My fellow classmates looked very good in their uniforms, but I thought I did not.

I was twelve years old when I started high school. There were about 80 students in our freshman class filling two homerooms at St. Anthony High Girls School. At Holy Rosary School, our graduating class consisted of 15 students. Now there were so many new faces to know. I wanted to meet them all. They were sophisticated and self-assured. My first year at St. Anthony Girls High School was difficult. Socially I was a misfit, and scholastically I was a dud. My awkwardness could also have come from the exposure to new acquaintances all at once. One could describe it as "culture shock."

I felt awkward attending this prestigious private school. Thinking back, I realize how petty my excuses were, but nevertheless they were excuses that stopped me from being happy. I was self-conscious about my uniform being too big for me. Besides my ill-fitted uniform, I noticed how the other girls took care of themselves. They used lotions and creams on their arms, legs and faces, and I could see that I needed some for myself, too. My skin was very dry and gray over my brown pigment. I used Vicks Vapor Rub since that was the only ointment I found at home that eliminated the dryness. I stopped using it when a classmate commented on the odor. Besides being an ugly duckling, I also did not know how to schedule my free time. During football season, I waited for my cousin for a ride home. I waited two to three hours after school while my cousin practiced football (therefore, not having enough time to do homework). I should have caught the bus back to Pā'ia, but the thought of riding with strangers was frightening (like my first bus ride in Honolulu).

The first time I rode on a public bus was when I was an eight-year-old with my Auntie Rose and Andy during a summer vacation on O'ahu. Andy and I flew to O'ahu to spend two months with our mothers' brother, Jose. Uncle Joe was stationed at Schofield Barracks and was married to Rose, a pretty Filipina from Pu'unēnē. We caught the bus early in the morning from their apartment at Red Hill Naval Housing in Moanalua to Downtown Honolulu. The bus carried people I never saw before—all kinds of faces. No one smiled. They were on their way to work with lunch cans in hands, or going home from work with tired eyes and rumpled hair.

117

A Maui Memoir

We got off the bus in Chinatown. The streets were congested with automobiles sometimes hardly moving because people crossed the street without using the crosswalks. The sidewalks were full of people. They shouted rapidly at each other in Chinese. Their conversations sounded harsh. I thought they were angry at each other, not realizing that this was how another language might sound. Pedestrians were serious about their shopping. They concentrated on buying the freshest vegetables and fruits, squeezing for firmness and sniffing for ripeness.

Vendors in the fish market wore white bloody aprons over sleeveless undershirts. They stood behind ice filled bins of whole fish, eels and crabs, waiting to make their next sale. Smells of the ocean was all around me and I felt wet and cold, but I admired all the different kinds of seafood. I was mesmerized by the scenes although I was careful not to lose sight of Andy and my aunt. I felt small in the crowd, worried that I would be left behind.

My experiences outside of Pā'ia were later limited to the weekend shopping trips that I took with my parents, aunt, or school. In grade school, I went on trips after school for sports competitions. It was a chance to see other kids, but interaction between us was limited. Each team glanced at each other through the volley ball net. I didn't make new friends easily. My friends were the people from my camp; we went to the same church and we played on the same roads.

At St. Anthony, my fashion sense was also forbidden by the nuns. I wore bright orange lipstick on my full and plump lips. Lips like mine were not in vogue at the time. I also wore lots of black eyeliner until Janet, the clerk at Segundo Store, told my aunt that I was too young to wear makeup. The nuns regulated the color of our lipstick. I could handle the color change but the habit of teasing my hair was tough to break. The bouffant that sat on my forehead was my creative expression. I thought I was a liberated woman in high school, but my thoughts were deflated along with my hair. Influenced by *American Bandstand* and the movies, I teased my hair at least two inches high and sprayed it stiff with Adorn hair spray. I thought I looked good. The nuns, however, made a rule against hair teasing. A few of us that teased our hair received an ultimatum to stop doing it or we would be suspended from school.

THEN, I lost my best friend. Mary and I were classmates since the fourth grade at Holy Rosary School, but she immediately made new friends at St. Anthony and spent her time with them and not me. She finally refused to hang out with me after I exclaimed, "Shit!" out loud one day in the parking lot. I was so hurt that she would alienate herself from me just because of that one outburst. A nun sat with me during lunch period while I explained to her between sobs of distress why Mary and I weren't friends anymore. Sister didn't give me much solace. She could only recommend prayers.

Cliques were already common in grade school at St. Anthony so the rest of us who came from feeder schools had to maneuver amongst them to find new friends. I didn't enjoy it, nor the challenging classes. I was not prepared to tackle the Algebra class that I was required to take. Each time I thought I had a formula, I did not. So I gave up trying. It also brought memories back of when my fourth grade teacher dared me to keep up with the rest of her class when I was promoted that year.

Although I loved to read and write, the English Literature class was boring and the classroom was too warm. It was also right after lunch. The nun who taught the class was frail and spoke softly. One of our assignments was to read a play adapted from *For Whom The Bells Toll* by Ernest Hemingway. It went over my head.

We had assignments in creative writing and simple fiction, but short romance stories were disinteresting to our teacher. She complained about the romantic tragedies that we wrote about. Well, at least we wrote about what was familiar!

Of the two offered languages to study, Latin intrigued me more than Spanish. Andy said Latin was the harder of the two, but it was the root of several languages. So I settled for Latin. As soon as we studied verb changes, I tuned out. Singing Latin hymns for years in our church choir didn't prepare me for Latin's complex structure.

Our religion class did not consist of questions and answers like we had to memorize in grade school. Now we had philosophical questions to answer that I barely grasped.

I wasn't doing well scholastically at all. I found that I left grade school without the maturity to deal with the demands of high school. It was an unpleasant experience, and I did not look forward to school anymore.

Socially, I did not fit in as much as I wanted. My first school dance date was with one of Andy's classmates. I rode to the dance with Andy, and I met my date at the dance. The cafeteria was decorated with crepe streamers and balloons. The lunch tables were folded and stacked against the walls. We danced, but he didn't make conversation. When the night ended and it was time to leave, he walked me to the car and opened the door for me. He knew some etiquette but he didn't say a word.

Then the junior class prom came around, and I was asked to attend by a very nice junior class gentleman. It was a treat as a freshman to be asked by a junior, but I declined because I thought he was too effeminate.

Nearly the end of the school year, I tried out for cheerleading, but did not make the squad. My girlfriend said I didn't smile enough.

I did not want to go back for my sophomore year at St. Anthony. Now I had to figure out a way of persuading my father to allow me to attend public school. But I had the whole summer to initiate a successful plan.

My transition into womanhood was quiet and undetectable. At the time, I neglected the signs thinking they were flukes somehow. I noticed brown smudges on my underwear but I didn't feel any pain or unusual behavior from my body, so I let it pass. I just thought it was from the tree branches we straddled while sitting in the trees. The smudges disappeared after a couple of days. But a few weeks later, they appeared again. This time, I casually mentioned it to Fely, saying that I didn't feel pain, it didn't have an odor but it reappeared again. That afternoon, Fely's mom asked me to go to their *banyo* with her. "I going show you something, Jackie," she said. Fely was too embarrassed to come in, so she stood at the door. "Why, wassa matta? You do this every month, too!" *Manang* Minnie said to her. "I going stay out here." Fely insisted. So *Manang* Minnie demonstrated how to adjust a sanitary napkin on to a belt the next time the smudges appeared. "Go home and tell your father that you need a box of Modess," she said gently. As soon as my father came home from work, and as he washed his *kau kau tin* at the sink, I embarrassingly told him that I needed to buy some Modess. After a moment, he nodded and said, "OK, we go." And we did.

I felt awkward in my body. One neighborhood boy teased me that I had a fat behind. I laughed as our chidings with each other were not meant to be vulgar. My waist and abdomen carried my excess fat and I didn't have enough breasts to fit into a regular bra size 28. No one told me that I was attractive, although when I looked at myself, I thought I was pretty. So when I had a "boyfriend" for a short time that summer, I thought I was in heaven.

He was a Portuguese boy who walked me home from a dance we girls organized at the Filipino Club House. My first kiss was on the front steps of my house. His breath smelled of fresh beer and cigarettes. He was just 15. I expected kisses to taste and smell like that from then on. Cool and slightly bitter.

About three weeks later, I found out that he was seeing another girl from Puʻunēnē. He sure made the rounds for someone that didn't have a driver's license. I had a terrible summer.

Tata Mitchell, third from left, accepting his
retirement gift. My father is standing in
the rear, fourth from right.

Last graduating class from
Holy Rosary Grade School '62.
I am in the first row, far left.

Growing Up Fast

"Slow down, you're trying to grow up too fast!" my fifteen year old cousin, Andy, advised me one day as he drove his mint green '56 Chevy to Dairy Queen in Kahului. "There's plenty of time," he said. I was discussing my heartbreak. In part, I was trying to catch up with the teenagers in our camp who were older than me by a year or more. They were sixteen and older, and I had just turned fourteen. I had more growing up to do.

Fely and I were too young to drive, so we depended on her older brother whenever he allowed us to tag along with him and his girlfriend. It was amazing how many of us fit in the backseat of their Datsun compact. If they went to a football game and didn't want us to tag along, we attended movies at the Maui Theater with Fely's mother instead. The fuzzy black and white Filipino movies ran weekly, spoken in a Filipino dialect no less. We watched the screen without subtitles and created our own plot. We were usually on the right track, and if we weren't, it didn't matter. It was something to do and we were out of the house, eating cuttlefish snacks, munching on Maui Potato Chips and drinking cokes in the Quonset hut theater that was across the road from the Bell House.

I decided to attend a Japanese film once, alone. I walked to the theater, hoping no one from the camp saw me. I wasn't sure if it was proper for a Filipino to attend a Japanese show. I approached the ticket window and

125

asked, "Can I buy a ticket?" The Japanese woman looked down from her stool and spoke through the hole in the window, "Of course you can." I gave her my quarter. A man at the door ripped my ticket stub and handed me my half of it.

The Japanese samurai film had already started when I crouched into a seat in the back row. I was astounded by the quality of the film. It was vivid with rich colors of the blue sky against the green forests. The countryside of Japan was so beautiful compared to the faded Filipino films. I tried to follow the story with the white subtitles but the printing disappeared into the background and the names were abstract to me. It didn't matter. I was mesmerized with Japan's countryside and samurai.

I attended the movies whenever I could, saving quarters for the admission. Most of the plots were difficult to follow and I missed most of the movies' purpose, but again it didn't matter. It was a self-education of other lives which resulted in happy endings. The unspoken message, however, clearly showed that white people were wealthy, and Filipinos and other Asians were hired as domestic help.

Movies were also my way of traveling. The cinematography offered a front seat to foreign countries that I could only dream of visiting.

As this summer was about to come to an end, it was again time to register for high school. Most of the teenagers in my neighborhood attended Maui High School. Andy and I, at that time, were the only two kids who attended St. Anthony's. Others had already graduated. I had to figure out how to convince my father that I ought to attend a public school rather than a private one.

Spirit of the Village

I approached him after his day shift and suggested the idea of transferring to a public school. He refused and was obstinate. His reason was that Andy was at St. Anthony and I should follow him as well. He wanted me to have a good Catholic education. But I nagged him, so he gradually gave in. The idea became favorable when I reminded him that it was cheaper to send me to a public school. I also told him, as a matter of fact, that I wasn't learning anything at St. Anthony.

In the main corridor of Maui High School, the registration line twisted from one end of the hallway, past the lockers and library, to the main office. My friends from the camp were surprised to see me, but greeted me with smiles when we stood in line to register. At last I felt that I belonged.

I felt more at ease at Maui High School, amidst the sugarcane fields of Hāmākuapoko. I caught the bus with Debbie and Flora at Nashiwa Bakery. The route to school was on Holomua Road above the Maui Children's Home on Baldwin Avenue. We made a left turn before the Makawao Union Church. We rode under dense foliage of wild plum trees bending over the graveled road. On the right side of the road, a big reservoir thick with mud was barely visible under all the leaning trees. The homes in Hāmākuapoko were already demolished. This was where the late congresswoman Patsy Mink lived at one time. By 1964, every inch of land around our campus was green and thick with lanky sugarcane. There were afternoons when the cane's silver tassels extended over the fields and pointed toward the sky, waving and spreading their pollen and announcing harvest time. The campus itself sprawled over acres lush with croton plants and flowering shower trees that shaded the lawns. In the main building, arched concrete hallways led to hardwood floor classrooms. The only noises were the buzzer between classes and our chattering while we walked to our classes or recesses. We were surrounded by sugarcane fields, mynahs and sparrows, and the occasional mongoose. Haleakalā Crater towered behind us and Ho'okipa Park knelt below us.

The bus traveled the route home along Hāna Highway above the white capped coastline of the Pacific Ocean and headed through Kuau. We turned left on Baldwin Avenue and went all the way to Nashiwa Bakery, dropping students off at intervals. The yellow bus emptied out by the time we reached the bakery. In all, it took about 40 minutes to get home from Maui High School. The ride was slow but pleasant.

Socially, my female classmates were friendly and cordial when entering the homeroom. One of the boys made occasional wise and inaudible remarks when a girl walked in and others laughed because it was the thing to do. Kids were from farms, ranches, and sugarcane or pineapple plantations. The ethnic mixture was a little of everything—Japanese, Chinese, Filipino, Hawaiian, Puerto Ricans, Portuguese and a small number of classmates whose ancestors were from Eastern Europe. I thought they were all Portuguese because they had fair skin. They weren't considered *haole* either, but we didn't distinguish one race as being better than the other. We did, however, tease each other and make jokes about our races, but everyone was easy to get along with. It was a treat for me to meet the occasional *haole* student who attended Maui High School, but they were mostly from transient families and did not stay long.

I noticed one odd thing though. Many Filipino immigrant students were placed in the Special Education classes. They were not mentally challenged, but English was their second language and they spoke with strong Filipino accents, having just arrived from the Philippines only months prior to attending school. They were very, very shy. Their separation from regular classes must have made them feel inferior. This was in the '60s and I never thought to question it.

Our teachers were mostly locals and others were *haole, kam'aina,* or *malihini.* Male instructors made up half of the faculty, a nice change for me since I always had nuns for teachers previously. I welcomed the mixed gender and appreciated this school system more than the Catholic one. Besides, there were so many boys to look at!

Needless to say, I enjoyed my remaining high school years at Maui High School. I reached my private goal of having fun through the rest of my high school years. With that in mind, I did not prepare myself for college. My designated future after high school was an office job, marriage and children, and that was as far as I could see. College was beyond my expectations.

As a result, I did not sign up for college prep courses, except for a senior literature class with Mrs. Mildred Bowen, a teacher with a tough reputation. Everyone thought that she was strict. But I thought she was an inspiration. She opened a door to William Shakespeare's world although I would not step entirely through it until much later in my life. She mustered excitement in reading *Macbeth,* so much so that I looked forward to her classes. One of our assignments was to recite a passage from *Macbeth,* either alone, with a partner, or with a group. Three of us chose the witches' scene. I used a stereotyped version of a witch who cackled too much; making use of cheap stage acting that I learned later was upstaging.

I concentrated mainly on the classes that provided business skills such as typing, accounting, and general business. I tried out for cheerleading, made the squad, and reveled in the popularity I craved for in my freshman year. It took the place of being lonely at home. Before I had my driver's license, my father drove and waited in the car for me during the football games at the old Kahului Fair Grounds on Puʻunēnē Ave. He might have attended the games, but he never let on if he did or not. He would have thought it was funny to see me trying to keep up with the football captain, Charlie Aruda, as we ran across the football field, hand in hand. Charlie was tall and also trained as a sumo wrestler. So imagine Charlie and me, barely five feet in height leading the team into the field.

My dad made sure I made it to the games whether or not he was tired from working in the fields. One time he nodded off to sleep at the wheel near Kanaha Pond before I shouted, "Daddy, Wake up!" I found him fast asleep in the car after the game was over.

I didn't have dates. The guys spoke to me in homeroom and classes. I had crushes on many of them, but I knew they were interested in other girls. I was asked out by a Filipino boy, but I refused because I didn't have a crush on him. I didn't know then that I didn't have to be in love to go on a date.

Eventually, I was able to ride to dances with my Japanese classmates that lived nearby, although their clique was difficult to break into. The girls that formed a club wore identical black and white outfits on Fridays. As I write this, I chuckle at the irony of wanting to be part of their group, but hating wearing the Catholic uniform.

I was liked. Besides cheerleading at all the games, I looked forward to our Junior Prom. The festivities included voting for the king and queen and their court. It also meant a date for the prom. Here was my chance to fulfill my childhood dreams of royalty. A queen and king and their court was chosen by popular vote. I was chosen as one of the court members. We picked our partners from the list of guys that were voted in, so I picked Eddie, a football and baseball athlete. He was sort of a rebel, but I liked his relaxed sort of style and he always smiled when he saw me. He lived in Nashiwa Camp. I also used to see him directing crosswalk traffic at Pā'ia School when he attended grade school. I thought he was a pretty laid back guy.

The weeks that followed included photo shoots for the yearbook. Our court dresses had to be sewn. It was much simpler for the guys who only had to rent white tuxedos from Gilbert's in Wailuku. And we had dance practice.

For five consecutive Sundays, we learned a tango, chosen by the group as our opening dance. Since I love dancing, I looked forward to practices in the school's auditorium called The Barn.

Not everyone shared my enthusiasm. Ed grumbled on the first day of dance practice; his excuse being, "Eh, but you some black!" I swatted him with a back hand across his shoulder. "No get smart!" I replied. He grinned and we became chums after that. He didn't have much choice for a partner, since we were both short in height. We would have ended up as partners anyway.

As the weeks went by, no one asked me to the prom. I patiently waited. Ed asked during recess one day, "Eh, I gotta take you, or what?" He was serious. I giggled. "No Eddie, you don't have to take me. You're just my partner in the court." "You sure? I no mind," he added. "No, you don't have to," I insisted. Besides, what about Sharon?" I asked him about his girlfriend who attended Baldwin High School. "She told me ask you!" I felt really pleased that they both considered the option. "No, you take her to the prom, Eddie." He nodded in response and continued, "You get one date?" I answered, "No." "Go ask somebody," he suggested. I wrinkled my nose, "Nah, I going wait." So I waited.

Ten days before the prom a classmate named Richard, a boy I barely knew, called and introduced himself. After both of us acknowledged that I knew who he was, he asked me to the prom. I accepted. He said, "OK, I see you later, then." I said, "OK, goodbye." "Bye." He hung up the phone, and so did I.

At the evening of the prom, my father had his camera ready to take a photo of me before I left the house. I liked the blue organza and white lace dress that we agreed to wear along with white gloves and blue-dyed satin shoes. I stood in front of the television set in our living room and posed for the photo. I think my father was proud. Minutes later, we heard a knock on the door and Richard was at our front steps. He introduced himself to my father and they shook hands. My father asked what time I'd be home. Richard said, "Before 12:00, Mr. Pias." It was all very proper being it was my first real date. I was concerned that my father would object that my date was a Japanese boy, but my father didn't mind.

We double dated with another Japanese couple who waited in the car while Richard came for me at my door. We made small talk, and that was fine since I was nervous about the prom—being on the court and being on a real date. Richard must have been just as nervous. We were both very quiet.

When we arrived at the parking lot in front of The Barn, couples were already flowing into the auditorium, dressed in semi-formal wear. Conversation and background music filled the air. I saw a spotlight swirling over the dance floor behind the front doors. We walked side by side through the parking lot and into the lit area in front. Just as we passed the hibiscus bushes and onto the lawn, Richard sprinted into the dark in front of the

Main Building and disappeared. Surprised and left standing there alone, I joined the rest of the Court assembling at the backstage door. I didn't see Richard again until after the tango when he reappeared next to me and handed me an orchid corsage. He danced well.

In fact, most of the students at Maui High School knew how to dance. For a P.E. activity, at least one quarter was dedicated to the basic steps in waltz, fox trot, sewing, rumba and cha-cha. We also learned basic etiquette of waiting to be asked or asking a partner to dance (when it was Lady's Choice). We also had a semester of roller skating. I preferred dancing to that. Besides dancing and roller skating, we were also required to play tennis, basketball, run laps, do long jumps and attempt the hurdles. At that time of my life, I deplored everything that required physical activity outdoors. But high school could not last forever, and I was also losing another friend.

A close friend, Barbara, who graduated from Maui High School that year, was moving to California. She lived with her grandparents in a bigger house across from the Pā'ia Gym, along the road that passed the Bell House, the theater and the clubhouse. I walked to her house from mine by accessing her backyard from the last row of houses that was on the edge of Orpheum Camp. She decided to move to California to get a better job and a new life. She was like a big sister to me during the previous two years. We shared our secrets and dreams. I spent the last of the summer afternoons in her pink bedroom listening to the songs of the Beach Boys and Barbara Lewis while she prepared for her night shift at the Maui Pineapple Cannery. I envied her for going away. California was a foreign world to me and the thought of leaving Maui was beyond my capacity. I didn't know how.

Abandonment, depression, and college were not words on my vocabulary list. I didn't understand why I was overcome with tears every morning when I woke up to Barbra Streisand singing "People" over KMVI Radio Station. I was always so melancholy—dreaming but not knowing how to turn my dreams into reality.

*

In 1965, a young policeman named Charles Maxwell, who cared about Maui's youth, sponsored dances in The Territorial Building at the Old Fair Grounds and at the National Guard Armory. He brought in live bands and encouraged teenagers to attend. Flora, Beverly and I attended them regularly. And that's where I met Norman, the boy who later said I didn't know how to boil water.

I recognized faces from other schools at these teen dances and met kids who attended Kamehameha School on Oʻahu who came home for the summer. It was a summer filled with dancing, meeting new people, and cementing friendships.

It was by chance that Norman and I saw each other on the dance floor. After the third weekend, I watched for him to enter the building. The feelings were mutual.

We became friends. He told me that he lived with his brother, his mother and grandfather in Wailuku. He brought me to their house to meet them. His grandmother had passed away before I met him but her photo was in the living room, adorned daily with fresh flowers from their yard. The roof of their house looked too heavy for the structure because it sagged and looked like it was ready to collapse at any moment. But it held up, even after the freak weather that dropped hail over

Wailuku one night. The plumeria trees and sweet gingers that surrounded the house were always in bloom. The scent was so welcoming.

Norman had a tightly knit group of friends who were hardly ever apart. They walked to and from school, worked and played together. In high school, he was a star athlete. Outside of school, he was a gambler. One of their favorite after school hangouts was Kameya's on Market Street in Wailuku. Although they were under age, they managed to drop their nickels into the pinball machines every afternoon on their way home from school.

Throughout our relationship, we frequently went out on weekends—six or seven of us, as many as who could fit into one car. Fortunately, one boy was old enough to drive, so we always had a ride to the movies or parties. They all pitched in for gas since they drove to Pā'ia from Wailuku to get us and then drove back into town to attend the Drive-In Movies, eat at Cupie's, or go bowling in Kahului or Wailuku. Then they drove all the way back to Pā'ia to bring us home before going home to Wailuku again.

I told my father about Norman. When I mentioned his full name, my father immediately disapproved. "Hawaiian, no good," was what he said. In those days, everybody knew everyone else, for how could my father detect Hawaiian out of Norman's Filipino last name? I was appalled. I didn't know my father had any prejudice towards other races.

I continued to see Norman although my father protested. We attended each other's proms, my senior prom at The Barn and his junior prom at the Wailuku Armory. Surprisingly, a lot of my classmates at Maui High knew him, since he and his family lived in Kula when he was younger. At recess the week after my senior prom, guys came up to me and said things like, "Eh, I know Norman. We went to school together in Kula." Or "Who you going cheer for at games, him or us?" Norman was popular, handsome and athletic at Baldwin High School. I was definitely in love.

My father did his best to keep us apart. One night while Norman and I were necking in his mother's car in front of my house, I heard an eerie cry coming out of the misty night. It might have been a cat in heat, but it sounded like a screeching, "Gooo home. . .." I felt uneasy. A tingling sensation ran down the back of my neck and I sensed danger. Moments later, a light shot through the windshield into our faces and the car door swung open on Norman's side. It was my father demanding Norman to get out of the car. As we both slid out of the car, my father pushed Norman away and shouted something at him. Norman shouted back. Then my father threatened him saying, "I going get my gun!" and rushed toward our house. I told Norman to go home. He started up the car, but before he drove away, he shouted, "You crazy old man!"

I was angry, embarrassed and totally surprised. In the house, I looked at my father standing in his silk maroon bathrobe, fumbling with bullets from an old cardboard box. I yelled at the top of my voice, "I HATE YOU!"

I thought I knew my father, his mild mannerisms and his quiet ways. I could not read his face to know if he was content or disappointed. His pent-up anger lay dormant until that night.

Events had changed him, too. His supposed lifetime partner had left him, and the threat of losing his only child was upon him.

We both calmed down as the days proceeded, but I was already stubborn and made my own decisions. Norman and I continued to date regardless of what my father thought. We managed to skirt around him, and Norman and I took it for granted that we would marry eventually. I was ready for the future that was destined for me. I did not wonder about whether I had other alternatives.

After that, time flowed as quickly as water out of a bottle. My insecurity and depression heightened when my father received his final warning to vacate our home. It was our turn to leave the camp for good. The families that could afford the down payment already moved to Kahului into the first increments of Dream City. The workers now had a chance to own their own homes and lot. The area chosen for them by the plantation was a hot bowl of sand that was undesirable for sugar cane production but good for housing development. It was something. "Better than nothing," the adults would say.

I watched my neighbors move away and I refused to say goodbye to any of them. I clammed up and went into denial. My closest neighbors, *Manang* Elizabeth, her husband and their children moved to Pukalani, someplace on the mountain where I'd never be able to visit. Some families moved to Kokomo. Each family, one by one, left one week or the next, and I shut the activities out of my mind. If my neighbors assisted each other with their moves, I wasn't part of it.

My mind was small then. The possibility of not seeing my aunt, cousin and uncle again was immensely disturbing to me. Their new house in Kahului was too far away. I had no means of traveling outside of Pā'ia, except with my father. We had no public bus service. Orpheum Camp was disappearing.

My father did not have the money to purchase a house and lot in Kahului, so we were assigned to another Store Camp, across the street from the Pā'ia Gym. I was relieved to hear that Flora and her family were moving to

School Camp near Pāʻia School. We were moving into unfamiliar ground even if it was just about a mile from our old place. In the past, we had no business in these other camps unless we knew someone who lived there—or if we walked through Nashiwa Camp on our way to school.

I rebelled against our move. "Why can't we stay here forever?" I asked out loud. I had lived here since my *hānai,* and it was my home. Why us, I wondered. We did not have any other choice. Inside, I felt that old stereotyped label of being Filipino and having the wrong skin color. One by one, each camp was eventually plowed under for new sugarcane fields except for Skill Village, which still stands today, with newly constructed houses scattered around the old.

One afternoon during the move, my father had his friends over after their shifts in the fields. They helped him move our furniture and paint the inside of our "new" house. He said that I should help paint, too. I grumbled. I was clumsy and insolent, and every time I turned around, the brush with brown floor paint slapped against the white wall. Or if I held the paint brush filled with white wall paint, I dropped it on the brown floor. The area that I painted took longer than if a more diligent person had done it properly the first time. It was a mess and I was impolite. I resented having to do it. The men murmured to each other in Filipino. Their posturing hinted as to what they thought of me. They lowered their eyes, turned their faces away and eventually ignored my presence. We moved in that weekend.

Our green upright telephone that I had ordered was not connected when we moved in. The black one at the old house was still in service so I walked through the abandoned neighborhood to use it.

Spirit of the Village

The camp was desolate. The mynahs squawked in the mango trees and the sparrows watched me from their perches on the telephone wires. Our homes were now wooden skeletons with gaping eyes and mouths that were once windows and doors. They exposed faded mint green walls, and oblong shadows where framed photos once hung. The taxidermy trophy heads of wild boar, mountain goats and winged pheasants that crowned a neighbor's living room walls were gone. The emptiness gave me goose bumps. The void was peculiar, but the sun was high in the sky and ghosts do not appear in daylight. Besides, I wanted to hear Norman's voice.

He was surprised to hear from me. He asked how it felt to be in an empty house. I described the empty kitchen to him and made my memories come alive. I saw the Christmas that my mom brought home a new puppy for my father. I smelled the shrimp and watercress soup steaming and the *dinengdeng* my mother cooked over her stove. My pink birthday candles were lit and ready to blow out at our kitchen table. My present was becoming my past.

Norman advised me to go home.

I heard Flora's voice in my mind, too. "Walk around the house and call out your name," she said. We had to call our spirits so they would not be left behind.

I stood up from the corner of the dusty living room floor. I walked into my old room which was once my mother's. Then I quickly entered the middle room that used to be mine as a little girl until my father took it. I whispered my name. Promptly, I walked into my father's old room. The shadows of the avocado tree waved against the barren floor and I immediately stepped through the dismal empty kitchen. I had made a complete circle within the house ending at the screened in porch. Chicken skin crawled up my arms.

Outside, I called my name again as I followed the path between the walls of our house and the garage. Images from warmer days emerged. My mother, in her blue cannery uniform dress, brushed against the clump of small Areca Palms every time she came out of the garage's side door, smiling because she was home from work. I saw my father asleep on his army cot under the eaves of the house because it gave shade and was cooler there in the afternoon when he napped before his night shift. I heard the chickens cluck and scratch the floors of their coops. I bid goodbye to the gnarled guava tree that once burgeoned with fruit. I squatted and peered under the house, something I used to do as a child to pass the time away, as if I might find a treasure of some sort. This time I saw just scraps of torn paper, fluttering from an invisible draft of air. A pigeon cooed in the distance. It was time to go.

I left Orpheum Village forever.

In our "new" house, the rooms were larger. An adjoining pantry in the kitchen had a window that faced the street. We made use of a screened-in cabinet, left from the previous tenants, to store our canned goods, flour and sugar. A smaller porch for shoes led outside to the street, but we closed that up because it faced the traffic. A window above the sink faced the road in front of our house and a side door led to the porch. The porch was quite big, extending from the kitchen, past the living room and to another bedroom on the other side. My father was not too keen about this bedroom with its own exit, or the bedroom nearest the kitchen. I suppose he wanted to keep me under surveillance, but it was already too late for that.

Spirit of the Village

There was an advantage to moving into this house. It had an indoor toilet, and the bedrooms had small walk-in closets. First, I chose the room with the bathroom and my father chose the one next to it. I later moved into the one next to the kitchen for more privacy.

To bathe, though, we walked out to a washroom between the garage and the house. It was bigger than our last one. The family before us left an old *tansu* that may have been shipped from Japan. It was built of very lightweight wood and not termite eaten. I used it to store my clothes.

We didn't make any improvements to the yard. A mango tree grew in front and a Chinese orchid tree grew opposite from it. The backyard was full of weeds. I hung our laundry on the line back there, avoiding the *kiko* that scratched my ankles or stuck to my pants.

Our German shepherd dog was tied up under the house. He grew to be a very big dog. He barked endlessly and the neighbors complained. My father eventually gave the dog to a family I didn't know. Later, I asked my father about it. "Dey eat 'im, I think." he replied.

Our new neighbors were Filipino, also. They had an adopted daughter, too. She liked to prepare a sweet dish of spaghetti with corn and sugared tomato sauce over white noodles. She often brought a bowl of it over to us. My father shared some of our food with them too, when he cooked more than we could eat. I didn't cook very much then.

On Sundays, my father gave me driving lessons since I was now 15 and able to get a driver's permit. He drove toward the Filipino Clubhouse and then stopped so we could exchange seats. I drove off the public road and onto the tournahauler roads in the sugarcane fields. I learned to steer our '57 Oldsmobile without worrying about other cars. I drove to Kehua and back. I practiced using the brakes and accelerator while steering that large automobile, sitting on two pillows. A few times I drove to Wailuku and back to Pāʻia, as my father cautiously directed me through sparse traffic on Hāna Highway and reminded me of the rules of safe driving. I took my driver's test in 1965 and passed at the first attempt. Flora had to take it twice. Unlike our car, hers had a standard shift. It was easy for me with an automatic drive to brake at the stop signs and step on the gas when it was time to move ahead, especially on the hill at High and Market Streets. The policeman who gave me the test was lenient, and only asked me to park in a diagonal parking space in front of the ʻIao Theater. He commented favorably about how I slowed down to the speed limit while driving up Vineyard.

By this time, most of my father's garnisheed bills were paid off. His paycheck was also heftier during harvest season. He bought a new VW Bug in 1966. The car was a challenge for me since it had a transmission with a stick shift. Its black exterior looked sharp against its red interior with a white overhead and black dashboard. It was an absolute cutie. I loved the smell of newness that lingered for the first month. During my father's night shifts, I practiced driving the Bug by manipulating the gears into place as I coasted down Baldwin Avenue, finding the right gear to accelerate at a decent pace. I drove to Wailuku to see Norman.

My father also gave me the money to splurge on clothes on his payday. I bought my clothes from Ikeda Store. The buyer had good taste for teenage fashions because I had a closet full of the latest styles pictured in the teen magazines I picked up at Machida Drugs. I was my father's "princess" no matter how frequently we argued.

Spirit of the Village

Soon, Norman and I, against my father's wishes, became inseparable. Norman's family didn't mind our relationship and they were cordial to me. I knew I was accepted the night his grandfather allowed me to dip my spoon into their family poi bowl. Prior to that, I always scooped poi into my own bowl with a serving spoon. I guess he assumed we'd get married at one point, too. But as Norman reminded me, if I couldn't boil water, I couldn't get married.

Their house in Happy Valley was just a one-bedroom house with an additional separate bedroom built closer to their outdoor washhouse. The house leaned over to one side and the kitchen floor sagged a little. The wood of the walls and floor was damp with moisture, especially in the evening. But soon was full of life, love and mischief.

Norman's friends assembled there almost daily and the beer parties on weekends were occasional, especially in high school. He took after his grandfather, Papa Joe, who was a rascal when he wanted to be, too. I wondered how Papa Joe kept his yard so green and in full blossom all the time. One day I found out. I walked through his yard and ducked my head under the low plumeria branches. The ground was filling with flowing water, like a taro patch. There was Papa Joe, at the edge of his property, lifting a piece of wood from the irrigation flume for the surrounding sugarcane fields. Water spilled out of the flume and channeled through Papa Joe's yard. That's how he watered his plumeria trees planted between the mango trees, ti and gingers. At night, the pungent aroma of plumeria with fresh ginger and sweet mangoes enveloped Pi'ihana.

I was a senior at Maui High School and Norman was beginning his junior year at Baldwin. The difference in years did not matter since I was still younger than Norman. There was no question of jealousy or anything to make a distant relationship fail. Actually, it was pretty fashionable to have distant relationships then. Some athletes at Maui High School had girlfriends that attended Baldwin and vice versa. One girl from Maui High had a boyfriend that attended Lahainaluna. I wondered how they managed dates; Lahaina being so far away!

As a senior, we had appointments with our counselors to review our status as young adults. The counselor looked at my papers one sunny morning, and asked me what I had in mind after graduation. Out of the blue, I said I wanted to go to college to study the humanities. He shrugged his shoulders and said, "You don't have the qualifications."

It occurred to me that my years in high school really turned out how I wanted them to be, loaded with fun and minimum study. It was time to think about higher education and I wasn't ready. I hadn't a clue that college could be as invigorating as Mrs. Bowen's class. Besides, we had no money for college.

The counselor had some solutions for people in my predicament. He suggested Maui Technical School for secretarial science, and sewing or beauty school on O'ahu. These were our choices. Beauty school was a good option. I took pleasure in styling hair, so that was a possibility I could endure.

At home, I discussed it with my father while he cooked our dinner. This was one of the few conversations between us that lasted for more that 10 minutes without an argument. All the while, he looked out the kitchen window, as he used to do in the old house, rinsing the rice or washing a dish. At first he did not like the idea of me leaving Maui. But after I told him that I could live with my cousins, Benny and his wife, he considered the idea. They replied to my letter with suggestions that were realistic but fearful. They said I could catch the bus from their home in Kalihi to the beauty college downtown. The idea of catching the bus was out of my comfort zone. I felt like I was being thrown out into the big ocean and had to save myself from drowning. I nixed the idea of leaving Maui.

The fear of riding the bus was burdening my dreams. Camp life kept me secure, but made me feel small and insignificant and unable to belong to a larger picture. This time, my father wouldn't be there to drive me to school.

Others from the camp did not have the same outlook as I had. Take my cousin, Andy, for example. In Orpheum camp, we did everything together. Being the older one, he watched over me ever since kindergarten at Holy Rosary School. We walked to school together. We spent our summer vacation on O'ahu together as youngsters, and I followed his footsteps to St. Anthony. When we went out with our neighborhood friends, he was also present, but he only gave me advice when I asked for it.

But as soon as they moved to Kahului, I lost daily contact with him. His parents supported his decision to attend college in California. Andy kept his good study habits and excelled in high school. My aunt told me her story about how Andy came home from St. Anthony's Boys School in his senior year and asked, "Ma, I can go college?" Not knowing where and how, Auntie Nora assured him, "Yeah, you can go." To pay his tuition, she worked in the pineapple cannery, and when she realized she could make more money in the fields, she picked pineapple. When her body couldn't take the bending and picking, she settled for hotel housekeeping, fixing beds and cleaning rooms.

Sometimes Andy did not make it home for the summer and other vacations because there wasn't enough money for his plane fare. Our mothers reversed roles. In California, my mother took care of his domestic needs by doing his laundry and cooking dinners for him when he stayed at her apartment on weekends. As for me in Orpheum Village, my aunt taught me the essentials of housekeeping.

My aunt's high pitched voice no longer threatened my absentmindedness after we all moved from Orpheum Village. Without her presence, I was never reminded of how I wasn't thoroughly drying the dishes, or how lazy I was because I didn't iron my father's working clothes. She sprinkle starched stiff denim pants, jackets, and long sleeved cuffed khaki shirts before she diligently ironed each piece. These were my uncle's work clothes. I obviously was not into that.

On Sundays, she ironed every piece of clothing that her family wore for the entire week. The list was long. At least three changes of thick denim clothing for my uncle, her uniforms and home clothes, Andy's uniforms and play clothes; not to mention my Uncle's boxer shorts, and undershirts that she made me iron in order to learn the craft of ironing. Even their pillow cases and crocheted doilies were starched. I ended up ironing them on Sundays in her kitchen.

She was, however, compassionate toward me as I grew older. Perhaps she too felt the responsibility for me lift by moving away. At the pineapple cannery where I worked one summer, she found routines for me that weren't so grueling during the shifts she had as a forelady. These jobs changed each evening. They were not

146

as monotonous as packing pineapple, one after the other, over an endless conveyor of yellow circles of sliced cooked fruit into thousands of aluminum cans. I was beginning to see some viable reasons why my mothers left Maui.

Every able female and male over 16 years old could have a job with the pineapple or sugar companies if they wanted one. Even if they didn't want it, they didn't have much of a choice. There wasn't much else to do except wait on tables or work in a department store—only if a relative or a friend had a position there for you. We carpooled from our camps and drove to the cannery in Kahului in our blue short-sleeve buttoned up shirts, jeans and white tennis shoes. We packed lunches of tuna or egg sandwiches, or rice with canned meats or leftovers from the night before. The cafeteria was not too expensive but our lunch break lasted 30 minutes with hardly enough time to eat, smoke a cigarette, and use the toilet. In the cannery's glove room, we gathered in front of the long mirrors to fix our hairnets and redo our lipstick. Our bango numbers were listed on a black board in case we had a day off the next day. Those days off grew seldom as the crops ripened, and the pineapple deliveries to the cannery arrived around the clock.

We poured talc into our yellow rubber gloves in order to slip our hands into them. Then the buzzer rang.

We were assigned to a particular row, either as a packer or a trimmer. As a packer, we dealt slices of graded pineapple into aluminum cans that clanked against each other on conveyor belts. Cannery noise echoed against the corrugated tin roof. Walls and concrete floors became slick with juice and water.

I was full of energy during the first week of work, with the thoughts of receiving a paycheck at the end of the pay period. I imagined the money I'd have at the end of the week. As the fourth week waned, getting up early in the morning, packing a lunch, and spending the day (or night) in the cannery were not fun. But there was no other place to work for an inexperienced 16-year-old person like me.

The day and night shifts at the cannery grew old fast. I had headaches and stomach aches and all sorts of discomfort. I made up excuses to stay home from work. Depression set in and I disliked everything about the job. Our shifts, during the height of the season lasted 9 to 12 hours at times. The overtime pay was good but not rewarding enough for me to endure. I cringed at the smell of pineapple and the scent of bad perfume stirred in with the constant noise of the machinery.

Cooked pineapple fused with the forelady's thin musk perfume. It gave me sinus headaches. The odor mixed with the ocean breeze that drifted through the high vents in the cannery. My nostrils burned from inhaling the chilly night air. Large and small aluminum cans bumped against each other, second after second, nonstop above our heads, traveling from the warehouses into the cannery on metal conveyors. The aluminum cylinders pulsed at eye level, one after the other. The glare from the cans came from the luminous downpour of artificial florescent lights. They were then sent down to flats on the conveyor belt in front of us.

The rumbling of forklifts and engines echoed off the cold concrete floors, and bounced against the corrugated skin of the cannery's thin walls, back down into my head. My feet, ankles and legs hurt from non-stop standing. I leaned against the steel sides of the coveyor and reached for the tubes of skinned pineapples that floated before us, ready for grading.

Each packer lifted a whole pineapple from the conveyor belt with middle fingers secured in the holes where the core was removed; one hand on each end, thumbs on the outside. We dealt each slice into separate cans separated in three groups—standard, choice and prime.

Standard, choice and prime. Standard, choice, and prime. We separated the pineapple out this way, all day.

Although I thought I had a pretty good eye that determined one grade from the other, my forelady reached from behind me and moved my slices to other grades. "Honey," she said, "'Dis goes ova hea." Her breath smelled of Chicklet gum, and her body oozed pineapple juice and the stale essence of her perfume. As she left my section and inspected others, she yelled above the deafening sounds, "Girls, no sitting now!" I never understood why we had these stools next to the tables. We were not allowed to sit on them during work hours. We stood from 3:00 p.m. to 3:00 a.m. one night. I quit the next day, but I had $142 in my bank account the following week. The next summer, I didn't work at all.

My mind dulled. I was bored.

A friend called about a dancing position in a hula troupe that performed shows for the tourists in the two hotels in Kahului. Auntie Hilda's Dance Troupe performed at the Maui Hukilau and the Maui Palms alternately. I learned the entire show in two weeks, and performed with the group the following week.

Dancing was a good escape.

Sometimes I wished that I had a large family with brothers and sisters because we would have each other for companions. On the other hand, I had an advantage as an only child. I had the family car to myself.

There were nights when I sped home from Wailuku after visiting Norman in Happy Valley. I raced across the Hāna Highway with only one other vehicle, a red truck filled with working men from the fields. It later

occurred to me that one of these men might have been my
father riding home from work.

I wonder what his thoughts were when he saw his
car speed past them at 80 miles an hour so I could get
home before him. Once, I denied everything when he felt
the car's hood after he came home, even though it was hot
to the touch. A disadvantage of being a spoiled child was
that I did not care.

As for Norman, he worked in the pineapple fields
during the summer and I did not get to see him unless I
visited him before he left home for his shifts in
Hali'imaile. His work was back-breaking, walking
between rows of razor-edged leaves of the pineapple
plants, bending to dislodge the ripen fruit, and throwing
it onto the truck's conveyor belt. He never complained.

For most teenagers then, it was a privilege to work
during the summer, as I realized later. But I didn't like
the hard work. Besides, my father always provided the
necessities, in addition to extras like clothes and
spending money. So what did I have to worry about? I
could have had this princess life all through adulthood if I
stayed in Pā'ia. I might have married and boiled water for
Norman, but it didn't happen that way.

After he graduated from high school, Norman
joined the National Guard and left for his six month
training on the Mainland. Others joined the military and
went to Vietnam. I had no concept of time, and I felt that
six months was a lifetime. I was restless. I dated other
guys before Norman's training was up.

Some nights, my girlfriend and I drove to Lahaina
and danced to live music at the *Red Eye* on Lahainaluna
Road. The floor was jammed with partners dancing to a
three or four piece band, depending on who made it to
work that evening.

Spirit of the Village

We were stopped at the door once by the owner of the club. He grabbed both of our arms at once, and took us aside. "Eh, what you girls doing here?" he asked. We gave him the usual local response—we shrugged our shoulders. "Dancing," my friend answered. "You girls too young, eh? How old you?" he questioned. We didn't answer. He shook his head, and a slight grin came across his lips. "Listen, you can dance here but if I catch you drinking, I call the cops, you hear?" We nodded, and said we only drank cherry cokes. From then on, we frequented the club without trying to disappear into the crowd, and hiding from his view when he occasionally showed up at his business.

Years later this man's handsome Asian face was plastered on the front page of *The Maui News*. He was the island's drug man, and was also indicted for gambling and prostitution. Fortunately, he didn't recruit us.

We met new people at the club. I had an encounter with a person I dreamt about. The person in the dream wore a pair of denim pants and white sneakers. Three nights later, I happened to look down the side of the person standing next to me, and there were those pants and sneakers. He asked me to dance. Cigarette smoke shimmied to the ceiling as I placed my cigarette in the ash tray in the middle of the table. The band rocked with Jimi Hendrix songs and the red lights over the dance floor flickered with the black light in unison. After a couple of dances with "Denim Pants," he took a chair and joined us at our table. He placed his left arm on the back of my chair and tried to fondle my left breast with his fingers. Shocked, I slapped his hand and said, "Hey, I am not that type!" He acted innocent and denied his actions. But after that he kept his hands to himself.

"Here, let's have a shot of tequila," he shouted over the music the following evening. "Oh, I've never had it before," I answered. Nursing cherry cokes did not impress this guy, I guess. "It's easy. I'll show you," he remarked. He ordered two shots of tequila, salt and wedges of lemon. The Red Eye was crowded as usual and the owner wasn't in sight.

I licked the salt off my wrist, sucked the lemon wedge and with puckered cheeks, I let the warm tequila slide down my throat. It felt like the liquid dug a trench through my esophagus by burning the sides of whatever it touched all the way down to my stomach.

While the rhythm guitar player lipped his microphone with the words to *Sunshine of Your Love*, the room became a caterpillar ride as it joined the whirling lights above me. My vision blurred, it doubled and my head spun. "Denim pants" led me out into the street and leaned my body against a parked car. "Are you all right?" he asked. I nodded. "I think so." He looked down at the side walk, "I'm sorry. I think that tequila was too strong for you." "Oh no!" I mumbled. "It was only that much." I fingered an inch of space between my thumb and forefinger. He sniffed air and plunged his hands into his pockets.

People sped past me. I shut my eyes to stop from weaving. The thought of spinning nuns crossed my mind.

I learned how potent tequila was after its effects subsided. Only then did I remember that he put a small pill in my palm early while at the club. I had taken it with my cherry coke before the tequila arrived. I think he said it was Mescaline. Someone said it was LSD. Whatever it was, at 3:00 a.m. that morning I was dancing barefoot down empty Front Street with a girl I knew from Kahului. Her name was Margie. I didn't see "Denim Pants" again.

Weeks passed.

Margie had met some hippies who rented a house in Makena. She wanted to visit them so she asked me to go along since I had a car. I was curious about how hippies lived, so this gave me a chance to see them in real life. They seemed carefree, and able to live in all sorts of conditions.

Stars and candles lit the lanai when we arrived. Someone picked on an acoustic guitar. Someone else said he was famous because he was once with the *Quick Silver Messenger Service*. Marijuana roaches and beer bottles littered the cable top table. I listened to them for what seemed hours under a *kiawe* tree that slouched over the lanai. Others just sat around. Some disappeared into the bush across the dirt road while others laid on the sand between the boulders on the beach. People hardly spoke.

We hung out for a few days. The women tolerated us. The men didn't think I was attractive. Maybe they thought I was still a child. But they liked Margie.

I would watch this sexually matured friend and them body surf in the nude. I wondered how the men kept their privates from being skinned, and how the women kept their nipples from getting raw when they came out of the white foamy sea. The smell of sex drifted in and out of the lava coves along the beach at night. I smoked pot but I kept my clothes on. I felt like an outsider again since the women were not friendly. They eventually left while we managed to hang out there for nearly a month. Every once in a while a new group appeared and the old group ventured somewhere else.

Early one morning, someone called my name and pointed to a rented car parked out front. I walked through the lanai and down the steps toward the automobile. It was a classmate home on furlough. "Hey Jackie, what's up?" he asked. I asked what he was doing in Makena and how he found me. He said he had called my father and my father directed him to the beach. I thought that was peculiar because I didn't recall telling my father of my whereabouts. My classmate said, "I came to bring you home." I was glad to see him, but I wasn't ready to leave. He drove off in his white car without me.

At 17 years old, I thought I knew just about everything. After all, I graduated from high school. My father and I consistently bumped heads, one more stubborn than the other, not agreeing on anything. One afternoon, I drove off without planning to return. I left without really knowing how to look out for myself. I was not concerned about money, because somehow it was always there. Fortunately, I "ran away" as far as Kahului, 15 miles from Pā'ia. To me, that was far enough to ignore interactions with my father. I decided to live with a woman friend I met at the Maui Hukilau nightclub and another girlfriend who decided she couldn't live at home either. One afternoon, she followed me to Pā'ia so I could leave our VW in the garage for my father. I left the keys on the kitchen table where he could find them when he came home from work. I found out how small Maui was when our apartment landlord told me to go home. He knew who my father was. Of course, I didn't listen.

I attended Maui Community College for two and a half years during its transition from a trade oriented school to a junior college. This was in 1966. I barely passed the required classes. I liked playing Hearts in the cafeteria instead. I enjoyed the social life over an academic one. I didn't think much about my future. Sometimes classmates who joined the military came home for their furloughs and came to the school. They quietly watched us play cards. I noticed one of them in particular was very quiet, unlike the way he used to be before he went to Vietnam. He left Maui with an innocent smile on his face, returned solemn and reserved, and finally he had no voice at all. I found his name, decades later, on the Vietnam Wall in Washington, D.C.

I looked for stimuli to kick-start my thoughts. I meditated in the morning on our front porch of our small apartment before I walked to Maui Community College. I signed up for the necessary classes, and waited for some kind of miracle to direct my course in life. None came.

Construction was not an issue at the time, but development on Maui had already begun. The first sign of it was when a vintage building in Wailuku was torn down for a nine story county building. The new monolithic block building with windows stood out over the New England type structures—a sign of the times. Rather than preserve Wailuku's charm, it negated it.

Haole students and teachers at MCC voiced their opinions about development. My first experience with activism occurred when one student wrote a paper for our Economics class and named it, *The Rape of Maui.* He asked me how I felt about it. I had no opinion, oblivious to how development was affecting Maui. Around that time, humanities instructor, Frank Tavares, gave a piano recital at the 'Iao Theater. During intermission, a Hawaiian woman came on stage and spoke strongly about Hawaiian Rights and how they were being taken away from the people. Her *haole* husband carried her off the stage. Months later, Frank formed a trio to perform in the hotels in Ka'anapali. I practiced with him as vocalist for a while but his direction turned from torch music to his own activist compositions. He had a short run at the Sheraton Maui Hotel when he sang about how tourism would ruin the island. Activism was over my head, and the changes came gradually and almost unnoticeable in my eyes.

I isolated myself from any kind of news. My instructors suggested I read the newspaper and magazines to stay in touch with the world and its issues, and to be informed with Maui's own changes. I found politics and development complicating and overwhelming. The bottom lines read, "We are killing people and for what?" "Why are we tearing down perfectly good buildings to build new ones?" I had plenty of thinking to do but no solution for a better world. I was busy in school, though, getting involved with the student government and hoping to learn more about administration and politics. However, college wasn't my sort of thing.

Soon, my roommate decided to return to her mother's house and I had the bedroom to myself. I had too much fun at night and had no desire to wake up the next morning for classes. Oblivious to the fact, I hadn't thought of paying a share of the rent until my other housemate suggested that I get a part time job. That was new. But I found a part time job at an answering service in Wailuku.

Moving out of Pā'ia was a breath of fresh air and freedom, although opportunities of becoming a worldly woman were scarce. Jobs were difficult to find, especially in Central Maui.

Hotels in Ka'anapali opened and I worked in the back office of Reservations at Sheraton Maui for a while. Just when I thought that I had maintained a decent hourly wage, I bought a new Hunter Green Karmman Ghia convertible. I suffered the consequences. Gas was expensive and driving to and from work ate most of my paycheck. The rest of my earnings covered the monthly payment for the car. I sold the car immediately and settled for an older sedan. I later quit the Sheraton and worked at the Maui Lu Resort in Kīhei, which offered a small increase in wages.

Junior Prom, 1965

Cousin Andrew Mark Quillope
St. Anthony High School, '65

Andy's dreams fulfilled
Mesa, Arizona

My Graduation from
Maui High School, '66
Hāmākuapoko, Maui

Spirit of the Village

Proposals

"How come Daddy wants to see me?" I asked my aunt.
She looked straight at me and answered, "Uncle wen find
one mate for your father." I didn't answer. "And we going
meet her at your father's house this weekend. He like you
come too."

Surprised but reposed, I sat at my aunt's dining
table and stared out her picture window. I felt a sudden
jolt in my solar plexus. My father remarrying never
crossed my mind. He had a short romance with a younger
woman years before, but that relationship did not
progress into anything serious. I was always the center of
my father's world, but now, he had an opportunity to
remarry. I thought my uncle was a traitor who didn't care
for me.

"Your father stay lonely, Jackie. He need
somebody." My aunt's voice shattered the void in my
mind.

A white sedan pulled up in front of our house in
Pā'ia at 5:30 on that Sunday afternoon. A couple sat in
front, and a woman sat in the back. My aunt, uncle and
my dad greeted the people as they stepped out of the car.
I stayed on the porch steps and waited until they
approached. The woman was very timid and walked

behind her brother and her sister-in-law, trying hard to be unnoticed. When we were introduced, she smiled and then immediately shied away, as if embarrassed about her own presence. I felt that she was very unlike my mother, who always faced the world head on.

In the house, we had some refreshments and then they resumed a conversation in *Ilocano*. Not comprehending this, I excused myself to leave. I was restless anyway and uncomfortable with these strangers in my father's house. I also sensed that this woman would take my place in my father's heart. The decision was quick. It may have been possible that he had been courting her for a while; I didn't know. But he asked to see me again and this time his ultimatum was disconcerting. "If you come home, I no get married," my father proposed.

There was a moment before I answered him, but I truly needed to make the right decision for the both of us at that moment. It meant his future as well as mine. The possibility of living with my father for the rest of my life did not settle well with me, although it is common in many local families. Images passed through my mind swiftly, picturing other father/daughter or mother/son families in Pā'ia. Security could also be smothering, I thought. I could not be both daughter and house companion to him. There was more to life and possibilities for me I felt, even though the chances of those on Maui were slim.

For once, I realized how deeply hurt and lonely he was all those years. Now, he really desired companionship for the rest of his life. However selfish my decision was then, it had to be the right one.

With certainty I answered, "No, Daddy. Better you get married. You and me, we only fight when I stay home." I left the house deeply depressed, but I felt I had made the right decision.

Their marriage was planned but I was not included as part of the wedding ensemble. I didn't attend the ceremony. It was my defense mechanism to avoid events when I felt insecure. The reception was held at Baldwin Park and many people came to celebrate their union. There was music, food and dancing. I stood in back of the outdoor pavilion, lingering under the trees, far from the lights. My girlfriend encouraged me to congratulate my father and his new bride, and to acknowledge my presence, but I could not. I felt I didn't have the right dress on. I felt that I didn't belong. I felt that I wasn't wanted. What I really felt and could not grasp was the severance from the lifelong tie with the one person who supported me during my entire life.

Brief Encounters

"What hotel?" my father asked as he gazed at their linoleum floor.

"It is called Guam Tokyo Hotel."

"Where?" he asked.

"Guam, Daddy."

He was quiet and pursed his lips. His wife, Ilang, intervened. "Good, Jackie, good for you. How much you get paid?"

"I'll be getting $150 a week, and they'll pay for my food and hotel room." I answered confidently.

Daddy nodded his head, "When you go?"

"Next week, Daddy." This was going to be my first trip outside of Hawai'i.

Sonny Knight, a popular 50's recording artist from Los Angeles and Chicago, mentioned my name to Ervin Groves, another recording artist, the week before. Mr. Groves needed someone to take his daughter's place in a gig that he had signed to do.

Previously, I had met Sonny at *The Office*, a piano bar in Wailuku where Bank of Hawai'i is now. Ed del Rosario and I walked in for a drink one night and sat at the piano. Eddie introduced us, and after a few sips of his beer, he chidingly said, "Jackie, sing a song." Cool Sonny played a few chords on the piano and then turned the

164

microphone in my direction. "Go ahead, Jackie, what would you like to sing?" I grinned. "Do you know *Dahil Sa Iyo*?" I asked.

In his slow and casual nod of his head, he chuckled. Of course he didn't. His warm personality beamed from his eyes smiling under his nearly closed eyelids. I felt comfortable with him right away. He answered, "Sing it for me." So I did. In five minutes, Sonny picked out the accompanying chords to my pitch, and we were doing *Dahil Sa Iyo* together for the first time. I sang two more songs with Sonny that evening, and many more after that.

Meanwhile, a really nice looking man arrived on Maui to teach karate at a health club that opened in Wailuku. It was the first of its kind then.

He had wavy golden hair and clear blue eyes. I was entranced immediately. He came in for a beer one afternoon during my shift at *The Office*. He said his name was Jimmy Carlin.

When Mr. Groves and I met for a rehearsal, we practiced thirty-three songs, twenty-seven of which became my immediate repertoire for Guam. The rehearsals continued for four more days, and then we were on an eight-hour TWA night flight headed for another little island in the Pacific. Ironically, somewhere on that island, lived my biological mother.

It was two weeks since I had met Jimmy for the first time. He brought me to the airport when I left for Guam and said he'd be on Maui when I returned in three months.

It was 5:30 a.m. at the Guam International Airport when we touched ground. I could not believe the blast of hot air on my skin when I stepped out of the airplane. I felt like I walked into an oven. We followed the

165

crowd into the airport, and I was struck by the amount of people there. They looked like me but they were different. People spoke in languages I did not understand. I was awed but waited for Mr. Groves' instructions. I was immediately homesick. Maui was not like this at all. Our airport was not like this either. We had a tree growing in the middle of the terminal with thousands of birds chirping. Maui people met arriving passengers with leis, hugs, and kisses. The breeze was cool on Maui and I knew where everything was. In Guam's airport, everyone rushed and crowded each other, and I couldn't find the exit.

In this terminal, I had no idea where to go, what to do, and it was really hot! People took up every inch of space, and no one was smiling. I was near tears and wished I had not left Maui. About that time, a man in a white short sleeved shirt and khaki shorts arrived and shook hands with Mr. Groves. I was also introduced to him. The whites of his two eyes stood out brilliantly against his black skin. He was the agent who booked the job for Ervin and Lani Groves, and was disappointed when he realized I wasn't Lani. He took us to the hotel, and suggested we rest since we had to start our contract that same evening.

There were two hotels on Tumon Bay in 1970. The Intercontinental was the other modern hotel next to ours. We drove through a circular driveway that led to the open-air lobby of the Guam Tokyo Hotel. The A-framed entrance had an interesting wood carving as part of the façade. Later I found out that it was a storyboard, part of the culture of the *Chamorros*, the indigenous people of Guam. The Chamorros looked Filipino, but after the desk clerk spoke to me in his native tongue, I knew I was an outsider. He was friendly but distant. I wasn't sure if I would make new friends. The thought of meeting my biological mother, however, was an event worth waiting for.

I wrote to her at an address that *Manang* Sising, her sister, gave me prior to my departure. *Manang* Sising and her children lived on Maui while her husband was in Vietnam. "It is an old address," *Manang* Sising said, "but try it anyway." I also had a telephone number that I dialed at various times, but no one answered. I also knew that she managed a bar in Agana, but I did not know the name or address of the place.

My singing routine at the Guam Tokyo Hotel started at 6:30 p.m. each evening and lasted until 9:30 p.m. My audience consisted of Japanese honeymooners, American servicemen, and United States citizens who worked on Guam, either at the hospital or construction companies. I was glad that I knew two modern Japanese songs because that was the only time I received a rousing applause from the Japanese couples. The servicemen from Andersen Air Force Base came to hear us. The U.S. professionals, doctors, dietitians, and project managers came to have their daily dosages of scotch and sodas, whiskey on the rocks, or San Miguel beers. I couldn't wait to get off stage. Being an entertainer wasn't what I thought it would be. It was boring and I was very homesick. I also missed Jimmy. About a month into the contract, Mr. Groves, with his parental intuition tried to improve my situation.

He arranged to get Jimmy on a plane to Guam. Mr. Groves knew how homesick I was and felt that Jim's presence might be good for me. His presence relieved my homesickness, but it didn't appease the situation that we were locked into for another two months.

He found a job to help with our living expenses. The contract that covered my food and lodging was no longer binding, and I had to pay for my meals and room after the second week that I arrived. I did not argue. I did not ask questions. I was brought up to accept all things that were dished to me without complaint. That was the mentality from the camp life. It did not work in the real world.

I was not impressed by the climate and topography of Guam. The flat low mountains of the island did not compare to the high blue peaks of West Maui. The dense concentration of coconut trees covering Guam's mountains looked forbidding and strange. They crowded each other, rampant with growth. I could believe the stories about Japanese soldiers hiding in these dense jungles without being found.

The cost of living in Guam was very expensive at that time, more so than Maui. $3.25 for a six ounce can of tuna was pretty astounding in 1970. We found living arrangements in a one-bedroom apartment with two United States Coast Guard sailors. They were stationed there for two years and patrolled the outer Marianas Islands to Truk weekly, which meant that part of the time they weren't at the apartment. That worked for a while, until one of them came home one afternoon and complained that dinner hadn't been made. He said that it was my responsibility to make it. But that wasn't part of the rental agreement. Words were exchanged, but from then on, he didn't speak to me at all. His roommate cared less whether there were meals prepared or not. He made his own.

Jimmy's job was delivering meals from the Guam hospital kitchen to the patients. Sometimes he worked nights. That worked out well since I also worked at night. Then we could spend the day together. Without a car we didn't see much of the island. Although our apartment was on the ocean, we didn't enjoy sitting on the beach.

The heat was unbearable, the ocean water was tepid and the sand bottom was covered with sea cucumbers. One of our roommates also told us that our neighbor kept a boa constrictor in a cage. I always wondered what I would do if it escaped. So we usually slept through the day in the air-conditioned apartment, and watched television. Sometimes we talked about my real mother, and wondered why she hadn't answered my first letter. I wrote another one to the same address and told her where I worked. But there wasn't a response. I gave up.

The time crawled by, and I thought my contract would never end. I didn't have friends my age, either. But Jimmy made one who was in the Air Force and a DJ for a night time radio jazz show. He also played the flute and came over after work and jammed. We listened to a lot of music. In between hits of ganja and hashish, he introduced us to Roberta Flack's album, *Reverend Lee,* and other blues and jazz albums. Jimmy and his DJ friend were into the music and getting high. I was into going home.

It was now November, and the last month of my contract. One night, a guest from Oʻahu was having his dinner in the lounge where we performed. He said he was on his way to Vietnam. I asked him what sort of business sent him there. He simply answered that some people made money out of war. He gave me his card in case I wanted a manager on Oʻahu when I returned to Hawaiʻi. I kept his card.

One afternoon, I had a disagreement with our agent and Mr. Groves. The agent wanted us to work extra nights at other clubs and insisted that we do so since he said we were bound to the contract. I refused. I lost my temper and shouted at the agent. "Mr. Groves told me that my food and my room would be taken care of, but it wasn't except for the first two weeks here. My contract didn't say we had to work seven nights a week either. Both of you lied to me!"

"Quiet down." the agent said.

"No, I will not!" I said and walked out of the room, angry and disappointed. I wanted to quit, but I needed to keep singing in order to earn my return plane fare home.

My animosity subsided after a few days. Several nights later, Mr. Groves asked if I would consider changing my mind, and join him in Japan to work another month in clubs there. By that time, I was disillusioned with a singing career. It wasn't glamorous as I expected it to be. It was difficult keeping my stage presence, entertaining with an unhappy heart, and keeping the audience satisfied. Being away from home was a major factor, too. I suppose if I wasn't so young, insecure and naive then, I could have made it as a club singer. I refused Mr. Groves' offer.

Our relationship did not develop into a close one, but Mr. Groves certainly had compassion, as it showed one evening during a very busy night.

A stranger stood at the glass doors of the dining room, watching us. I couldn't see the person because the lights illuminated her body from behind, casting a shadow on the face. Mr. Groves and I didn't think anything of it, since lots of people just stand at the doorway before they decide to come in. During our next break, I went outside and sat at one of the round glass tables next to the pool. The lights in the pool made the aqua water shimmer against the dark ferns and palms of the hotel's tropical garden. The reflection stopped time as it flickered against the glass table.

"Jackie," Ervin called from behind me. The stranger was standing next to him. "Say 'Hello' to your mother."

The next thing I heard was, "Ask her to sit down, Jackie. Go ahead and talk. Come back in when you're ready." He pulled a chair out for her, and then returned to his keyboard onstage to start the last set.

My biological mother sat across from me, her palms opened and extended to me. "Jackie, I came back for you, but they wouldn't let me take you." I looked at this woman and recognized the forehead that our family genes produced. My cousins, Vivian and John, have it. I have it. I had no doubt that this person was the woman who gave birth to me. I touched her hands, and let my head hang with relief, reunion and mixed emotions. We held each other and cried for a very long time.

She picked me up the next day in a brand new white sedan and drove me to a house in a local neighborhood. She went into the house and came out with two little boys. She introduced them to me as my brothers. While she brought them back into the house, a stranger approached me with a little girl and said that this little one was also my sister. I didn't know who the man was, but he and the girl left before my mother returned to the car. We drove away and I told her what just happened. She shrugged and laughed it off. We didn't discuss it further. My habit of not asking questions created a lot of mystery in my mind.

I saw her two more times. The first time, she brought Ervin and me to a club that she said she once managed. A full orchestra of Filipino men played there, and the customers were mainly balding men who sat in dark corners. I wasn't impressed with the surroundings. She surprised me and came out with a cake that said, "Happy 21st Birthday to my daughter, Jackie." The band struck up with *Happy Birthday* and everyone in the bar sang to me. She was proud. She took me aside and said, "I bet you never had a cake for your birthday." "No," I answered. "My mother gave me one when I was seven." If Ervin had heard my remark, he didn't respond. He stayed composed and did not say much that evening.

Later, I asked Jenny why she had not responded to my letter sooner. She said she had not received it, although she had heard that an entertainer from Maui was searching for her mother whose first name was "Jenny." She was called "Jenny" on Maui; but on Guam, people knew her as "Virgie." We planned to meet once more before it was time for me to leave Guam. I waited for her to call or come by. She did not, and I left Guam with a scarlet sunset behind me. Jimmy had already returned to Hawai'i, and I was to meet him in Honolulu. I was almost home.

Not Quite Home

Two days after I arrived in Honolulu, I called the number on the business card that the businessman in Guam had given me. He arranged to get a job for me immediately. His two partners, a man and woman, bought a crimson polyester evening gown for me to wear and brought me to various Waikiki shows in progress. They introduced me to Trummy Young, Danny Kaleikini, and Paul Conrad. I got up on stage and sang two songs with each of them. With hardly any stage presence and confidence, I sang with these well known entertainers for a night. They were very congenial and gave me advice. Mr. Young said it was a hard business to be in, but to keep at it. Mr. Kaleikini wished me good luck, and Mr. Conrad gave me a condescending grin.

I also made a demo tape that week. The partners hired some studio musicians and I recorded with a raspy voice, filled with phlegm from smoking a pack of Winston cigarettes a day. I was offered a spot in a small piano bar in Waikiki to get "more experience." I went to see the room. It was in the basement of the hotel; fake palm trees in the corners, cigarette smoke rising between the yellow and orange spot lights. The room was so narrow there were barely places to sit except around the piano. The sound system was bad compared to the perfect one I had in Guam.

173

A Maui Memoir

The next day I made reservations for a flight to Maui. I phoned one of the partners and told him, "When you find a better room, call me. I'll be on Maui."

He never called.

Jim and I lived in our friend's small RV for a while. We moved it from here to there in Haiku, parking alternately in friends' front yards. During the rainy season, it became miserably moldy and cold. Eventually we moved in with his close friend from his hometown in Alabama. His friend had a house in Pukalani but was going through a divorce. We lived there for about a year before the divorce was finalized and the house was sold. That's when Jimmy decided to buy an old International truck and live on the beach.

By that time, we had accumulated some possessions—two cats, Buster and Mahalia, our clothes, and a cast iron Dutch oven that belonged to my maternal grandmother. With the possessions in a holding box built into the back of the International, and the cats with us in the cab, we moved to Mākena under a grove of *kiawe* trees overlooking an entire stretch of white sand beach with not a person on it. We lived there undisturbed for an entire month.

I should have enjoyed that experience, but I didn't know better. I hated living on the beach. I did not know that camping at choice spots such as that one would be the last time for anyone. My expectations were very materialistic, and living out in nature was the last thing I wanted.

On the other hand, weather conditions were beautiful. It rained once. The ocean was flat and calm in the morning, choppier in the afternoon, then flat again as the sun set between Kahoʻolawe and Lanaʻi. Some friends came and camped for the night. Being an island girl who hardly played on the shores of Baldwin Park or Hoʻokipa, this homeless life was uncomfortable to me. I did not know how to swim either, so days that should have been leisure ones soon became tedious. So I sat on the beach knitting, crocheting or reading.

The cats played in the weeds, caught mice, and slumbered in the afternoon shade. They loved being there, and so did Jimmy. An avid swimmer and skin diver, he figured out a way to earn a living during our homeless hiatus.

He went into Happy Valley in Wailuku one day and bought a fishnet from Valley Isle Hardware. It was about 25 feet long and made out of monofilament, with lead weights attached to one length of the net. Every evening before dusk, he folded the net accordion style, draped it over an inner tube, and paddled out from shore. As far as I could tell, he dropped one end of the net closer to shore and laid the rest into the water as he swam outward. Empty bleach bottles were attached to each end of the net, serving as floaters and markers. Then he'd paddle back in with the tire. He asked me to go along with him, but I was adamant about going into deep water.

Our dinners were cooked over a *kiawe* wood fire. During an overnight visit, Mei Ling Chang, whom I worked with at *The Office* before I left for Guam, showed me how to bake biscuits in the black cast iron Dutch oven. She mixed some dough and placed it in the greased pot and put the lid on. She dragged the hot coals aside to make a shallow hole and then laid the pot into the hot sand and surrounded it with the coals. About 10 minutes later, the biscuits were done, piping hot and delicious. The pot was a valuable asset for my stint as an outdoor cook. I made all sorts of suppers in it—stew, chicken hekka, or curry. Otherwise, we grilled the fresh fish Jim

175

caught over the open fire, under the endless, star studded sky of Makena. Every night, the campsite was peaceful. We slept comfortably on air mattresses in the bed of the truck. In the mornings, I boiled water for tea over the open fire.

At dawn, just before colors appeared in the sky, the water was motionless from the windless night before. Jimmy already had on his swim shorts, snorkel, mask and fins and swam out to his net. He had gathered the net, starting from the deepest end, laid it over the tire until the entire length draped over it. As he pulled it into shore, bits of sunlight sparked against the bodies of fish entangled in the net. Occasionally, the fish escaped the net which left gaps between the knots. Jimmy drove to Pāʻia to learn how to patch his nets from *Tata* Poro who threw net when conditions were good.

Usually, Jim's net was filled with *lai* and *weke*. Sometimes there were just a few. One day, Jimmy's best friend, Scott Johnson, visited us. They met at the University of Hawaiʻi at Mānoa when Jimmy attended school there. I was still asleep in the bed of our truck, and Scott was on the sand in his sleeping bag. I heard Jimmy shout, "Whoa!" from off shore. The water was glassy flat and gray like the sky. I looked up and saw him wave at Scott to join him.

When Scott reached Jimmy, I could hear their voices drifting over the water to the campsite. They were discussing something about the net. Scott shouted out, "Jackie, you ought to come in." Yeah, right. "No, no thanks," I shouted back. Jimmy dove into the water once more, and emerged to the surface with a huge tail fin in his hand. Eerie as the ocean was—silver, flat and still—the fin was even stranger. It extended beyond Jim's facemask. From where I sat on shore, the fish looked monstrous. They swam in, Scott with the tire and the net, and Jimmy with his catch. The water quivered slightly in the wake that they caused.

He dragged this magnificent fish, with large round eyes, and a long slim and steel-looking body, from the water onto the shore. The fish had swum directly into the net and wrapped itself with it when it struggled to get away. The other fish looked like tiny babies next to this one. On the cold wet sand, we untangled the smaller fish, releasing their gills from the monofilament and placing them in the coolers filled with ice. Jimmy and Scott left immediately for town to sell the catch to the fish market. I jotted notes down in my black journal while they were gone.

The people at Noda Market identified the big fish as an 'Ō'io. Since it was a bony fish, it was only good for making fish cakes, they said. But they paid a good price for it and the rest of the catch, thus making it the biggest sale for Jimmy, the fisherman.

He swam out into the ocean to spear kūmū, uhu and squid for our dinners. Swimming deeper, he'd come in with pāpio and once, an ulua. On the other side of the island at Paukūkalo, he'd pick lobster during season. With vegetables, poultry and meats that we bought, our diet was sufficient. We ate quite well. No rent, no bills. We faired well, except that we didn't have a roof over our heads.

One day, someone in a land rover drove up to our campsite, but stopped before getting too close to our site. He got out of the automobile as Jimmy approached him. They spoke for a while. Then he turned to look at the campsite and me. He smiled and then left. Reluctantly, Jimmy shared the news. A resort was taking place and we would have to move. Jimmy shrugged his shoulders, and said we would wait until someone came with a bulldozer. This was in 1971 and I was twenty-one years old.

The man came back a few weeks later and told us again that we HAD to move. We reluctantly packed up and re-located ourselves at Nu`u Bay. We didn't last through the night. The waves crashed against the huge boulders and the wind blew fiercely. Rocks burst from the heat of the campfire, acting like missiles flying between the cats and us. We packed immediately and drove back to Mākena, slept there for the night, and drove into Wailuku the next day. We stopped at a friend's house and asked if she knew of a place to rent.   She said she had a basement that we could move into.

The basement apartment was the first home we shared with a roof over our heads. We used an old door for a kitchen counter, our Coleman stove for cooking, and propped a side of a telephone cable spool on a wooden box for our dining table. We sat on cushions to eat. Shortly after, we purchased a waterbed.

I found a job serving cocktails at the famous late night dive in 'Iao Valley; not coming home until after the last call and our *pau hana* drink consumed at 3:30 a.m. Was this a sort of life that my mothers before me tried to avoid?

While I worked in the evenings, Jimmy played with some candle wax and made his first sand candle. We formed a company making sand candles, and sea urchin candles. Meanwhile, I learned to cook and bake on our Coleman Stove. I even made a mango pie for Jimmy's family—seven women from Alabama—aunts, friends and Jimmy's grandmother.

Jimmy flew to Honolulu to spend time with them, and then they booked a flight for me to join them. Still a novice at traveling, I grabbed a taxi from the airport to Waikiki and told the driver to take me to the Edgewater

Hotel. He was curious about my destination and asked, "You meeting somebody over dea?" I responded favorably saying that my boyfriend and his family were waiting there for me. The driver turned around and said insistently, "You *sure* das whea dey stay?" I said, "Yes, it is."

When we arrived at the Edgewater, I realized why the driver was so reluctant to bring me there. The hotel was not the kind of hotel that women from Alabama would book themselves into. At that moment, I realized that I had given him the wrong hotel name. I was supposed to go to the Outrigger East. Edgewater. Outrigger. They almost referred to the same thing—ocean! Names were meaningless to me; I didn't think it was important to remember the right one. The cab driver was relieved.

I arrived at the correct hotel two hours later than expected. Jimmy was worried. His grandmother came out of her bedroom and gave me a great big hug when I entered the hotel room. "We were worried about you, Honey!" I knew at that moment that I was accepted into his family. We stayed with them for a couple more days.

After we left, the entourage was scheduled to be on Maui for a day, so I made a fresh mango pie which came out of the Coleman oven just before their visit to our basement apartment. They were amazed. The pie was consumed within minutes.

During the next few years, Jim and I made sand candles for a living. In 1975, we married. Scott was our Best Man and my mother, Rose, was our Matron of Honor. In 1977, we had a daughter, Puacita.

I did not hear from Jenny for many years following our first meeting in Guam.

Some Mo'

In 1978, my husband, James Andrew Carlin, committed suicide. He was thirty-one years old and I was twenty-eight. I screamed, swore, and cried when I heard the news. After the initial shock, my nerve ends went numb for the entire day. My hearing changed. It felt as if I had cotton balls in my ears, muffling voices and sounds around me.

My brother-in-law, Ron and his wife, Julia, flew from Alabama to attend Jimmy's services. Joe Bulgo from Bulgo's Mortuary, remembering my father, personally arranged the proceedings for me. If it wasn't for his advice, I would have spent more money than was necessary.

We picked up Jimmy's remains in a carefully wrapped box. It was against his mother's wishes. She wanted his body sent to Alabama. However, Jimmy and I discussed his wishes long before his death occurred, interestingly enough. I stood my ground, although I knew it was against Catholic beliefs and Filipino superstitions.

I felt sick on the day of the scattering. I didn't want to get up from the pune'e in our living room. Sheila called my doctor. He said I was hyperventilating and advised me to breathe in and out of a paper sack.

The box with Jimmy's remains was heavy.

We scattered his ashes in Ma'alaea Bay. Bob Hein powered a rubber Zodiac off shore in order to do that. Bob, Sheila Franck, John Roberto, Will Griffis, Ronnie

Spirit of the Village

Carlin and I huddled together in the boat. With hopes of a supernatural sign, I mentally asked to see a dolphin. As I watched toward the horizon for one to appear, my friends faced the shore, not knowing what I was praying for. All of a sudden a friend shouted, "LOOK!" Behind me, a dolphin leaped out of the water. By the time I turned around, it went under again and glided through the circle of flowers that we dropped over the ashes.

I had an infant daughter to care for and I knew how to boil water, but the life lines in my palm did not prepare me for a spouse's early death. It was a drastic turning point, and our survival depended on my decisions.

One thing for sure, though, is that I had family. My biological aunt, *Manang* Sising and Papa visited me on two separate occasions and offered their help. My grandfather offered his house to my daughter and me if I wanted it. He said, "I no can take care you before, but now I can, you and your daughter." My father and stepmother, Ilang, patiently stood by as I went through my periods of anger and disappointment.

Norman, back from O'ahu and recently married, came to visit and asked how things were with me. He wanted to be sure that I was all right. We are good friends, even now.

My friends hovered over me like angels. After the suicide, I decided to stay in the play, *South Pacific.* I was *Bloody Mary.* The play was performed in the Territorial Building at the Old Fair Grounds. Jojo Apo and Colleen Reilly stood by me in the wings before the curtains rose, reminding me that the proscenium was a good place to leave my grief behind—while I became another person for the stage—legitimate for stage performance. Bob and Sheila made sure I ate and slept well. We mourned together. Jimmy's death was tough for everyone. In October of the same year, my father passed away.

The sounds of my father's music floated out of the village, too. On the day he died at his home in Kahului in 1978, my *hānai* mother in California said that she heard him sing in the distance. I thought her neighbor's stereo might have triggered her memory. But the song and the voice were familiar to her because he sang, *"Dahil Sa Iyo...."* the first song I learned as a child. At my father's funeral, I wasn't sure if I was grieving for my husband or for him. He died only six months after my husband. I learned that it takes longer than six months to get over a death, let alone a suicide.

In my dad's wallet at the time of his death, there was a photo that he kept with him all those years. It was a picture of me at my 1st communion. I stood at the altar of Holy Rosary Church in my white dress, veil, and patent leather shoes and lacey anklets. I held my prayer book before me, displaying it to the camera. I had a broad smile on my face. I was proud and happy then. In his closet, the shirt that I sewn for him a long time ago was still part of his every wardrobe.

My mother, Rose, died in 1985 in California. My aunt, my daughter and I traveled to California for her funeral and burial. Andy was her executor and asked me to help him find her bank documents and other papers. He looked for them previously but could not locate them. I agreed, not really thinking of any particular place to look first. But the subconscious works in mysterious ways. I saw her closet and her night clothes, and I unconsciously slipped my hand in one of the pockets of her coats. The documents were all there.

Spirit of the Village

As a child, I often saw both my parents hide their cash and valuables in the closet, in the pockets of their favorite coats.

I also looked around for the many pieces of paper on which she might have written. I came up empty except for a small 2" x 3" notepad which contained a letter to her Dutch ex-husband. The pages capsulized her passion and anguish. It baffled me that this was the only evidence of her writing. I saw her writing constantly when she lived with us, and I wished I had found more.

My biological mother, Jenny, returned to Maui twice after Rose passed away. Both times I've asked her about her past in the attempt to get a grip on mine, but her stories were always vague.

* * *

I was present at Kula Sanitarium the night my grandfather died. His daughter, *Manang* Sising (Rosita Balios), and her children surrounded his bed. Although he was incoherent, they arranged his pillow, dabbed his lips with cool water, and spoke words of comfort and love close to his ears. They did not leave his side until after he passed on.

Many of the people I mention in this book are now in spirit, also. My best friends in Orpheum Village, Beverly Martin Rodrigues and Flora Medrano Pagaduan have passed on. My Uncle Aning died in 1998. My aunt lives in Kahului and Andy lives in California with his daughter, Michelle Quillope.

I have never met my biological father, Isabelo Galima.

Mabuhay

It was memories from my camp life that gave me a sense of belonging to someone and some place. Sometimes they came in the form of images from my childhood such as the evenings I heard my father and his friends serenading at midnight on Christmas and New Years Eve throughout Orpheum Village. I could hear their music from across the camp and into my bedroom. He told me that in front of each house, they'd play a song. Some neighbors already had their porch lights beckoning them to stop at their homes. The group then played two or three songs and the neighbor came out to give them coffee and treats or a monetary gift. Then the band would continue down the road.

I envisioned them playing in the dark, offering their gift of music to the camp. As if I was standing outside with them, I saw *Tata* Olong, Daddy, and their friends recreate their hometown custom. The sound of my father's saxophone in the night made me warm inside. Then the music would melt away, and I would drift to sleep. This was where I used to live, with the heartbeat of music everywhere.

The transition from their homeland habits to new ones was not easy. My uncles used to sit at the dinner table, one foot propped up on the chair so their knee pointed upward. One elbow leaned on the table so the other hand could be used for eating. They formed the hot rice into a small ball with their thumb and first two fingers, sometimes adding small bits of meat or vegetable with it. Neatly packed and held between the thumb and the fingers, they brought the food to their lips and then pushed it into their mouth with their thumb. Dinners at home were the only times that my uncles practiced their cultural way of eating—with their fingers.

I tried to copy them, but I made a mess of myself and the table. My mother forbade us from eating with our fingers. We were civilized now.

Filipino laborers migrated to Hawai'i after the groups from Asia, Europe and South America. When Filipinos first appeared on Hawaiian soil, they were regarded as men with childlike minds. They were treated badly and an inferiority complex developed and traveled through the veins of posterity to produce individuals like myself. As I was growing up, I spent so much time learning how to be *haole* rather than to be Filipino. Being *haole* represented success, wealth, and superiority.

But that was my own viewpoint, and the children next door to me probably did not share the same feelings about themselves. Each house, despite the stamped-out look of our dwellings, had its own dynamics.

My teen years with my father were tumultuous. I was hardheaded and thought I knew everything. Of course I must have, since I was almost out of high school and my father was only a dumb laborer in the fields. It never occurred to me that he was an educated man like his brothers, and he had emotions like I did. He never complained about his work in the fields and how demeaning it might have felt to be treated rudely because he was Filipino.

We did not discuss how we felt after my mother left Maui for California. I am sure that his thoughts were filled with confusion, sadness and doubt, like mine were. I can only measure his feelings of losing his own wife against my own pain of losing a lover. He stood by me as I grew into a woman. He had the patience of a saint. He was always there for me even though I was not his biological child. And even that is not enough to realize the loss of hope and dreams he had for me, and maybe for himself.

He often told me, "You teenk you know everything now. Wait wen you grow up, den you find out."

Uncle Aning dancing, *Tata* Poro in the
striped shirt standing, and Papa with the
white baseball cap laughing.

My First Holy Communion
Holy Rosary Church

After-Thoughts

Through vivid memories, I return to Pā'ia often. It seemed that the only way I could get peace of mind was to write these images down and let them relive their days. By doing so, I managed to unknot the many tangles of my childhood.

Writing an autobiography is a continuous process of discovery and rediscovery. I could rewrite this memoir many times and arrive at a different outlook about the events and people every time. This book is a result from my viewpoint, and I hope that others will write theirs down to express theirs also.

I often thought that our relocation and the demolition of my neighborhood were what caused my listlessness and directionless, loss of stability and sense of place. But there is no one to blame. By writing, I was able to organize my memories and notice the people who were around me and how their influence affected me as a child. Writing about my past gave me an opportunity to forgive—myself and others.   I really had to know my own history before I could move forward.

After every rewrite, the purpose of my memoir became obvious. It cleared a lot of doubt. The 50s in Pā'ia was a time when we did not have the education to recognize depression, or abandonment issues. It was a time when opportunities were hard to come by. In reality, I wasn't abandoned like I thought I was. I had my *hānai* family, and a network of extended families that took the places of my biological parents. My mothers had to find what was best for them, even if it meant leaving family and friends they loved.

I also outgrew the prejudice I had toward *mahu*. It was a learned thing, making fun of them. We grew up with *mahu* in the camps and in high school, although we didn't use that term at the time. I don't think we understood them. Unfortunately, some of our friends eventually died of AIDS, too.

For the reader, this book offers a glimpse of what plantation life was like in a Filipino Camp. It was probably similar to yours, or possibly very different. Plantation life in Hawai'i is part of the past now. But for many of us, it is our roots.

When I turned forty in the late 1980s, it was uncomfortable for me to hear about the blood quantum issue of Hawaiians. While native Hawaiians measured how much Hawaiian blood they had, I wondered where I belonged with no Hawaiian blood at all. I was born in Hawai'i, not the Philippines. What culture do I belong to? As I write, I believe I have inherited them all.

Since 1983, I have met some of my other siblings. We share a biological mother and they too are curious about her. At the last count we are nine in all. They were brought up by their military fathers who were stationed throughout the world. Our biological mother died on Guam in November 2005.

Spirit of the Village

From 1972 to 1992, I worked as a self-employed crafts person, artist and stage actor and received awards such as "Kittys" from the Maui Community Theater, and selected for Art Maui and Hawaiʻi Craftsmen. During this period, I also served on the Maui Historical Society Board, held an interim director position for the Bailey House Museum, and served two terms on the Board of the Hawaiʻi Council on Humanities. In the late 90s, I was a member of the Maui County Cultural Resources Commission, and concluded my term as Chairperson of the Board. It was in this commission that I saw the two sides of every issue. My decisions were and still are pro our host culture.

Between 1992 and 1997, I went through female empowerment—menopause. I mention this because this was when I gained the strength to reshape my life. My daughter was finishing high school, preparing for college, and I had been thinking about my own future. I was not enjoying being an artist anymore. I sold my belongings, moved out of our rented home, and dropped out.

During that summer, I lived with friends in Portland, Maine, hoping to "find myself." When I left Maui, I vowed never to paint again—except that I did bring a watercolor pad and paints with me, just in case.

Never say, "Never." On a quiet and clear morning, while painting water lilies on a Damariscotta Lake dock, I had a revelation. I realized that it was not in my power to reject my talents. I should not doubt them, either. Not every project turns out to be a masterpiece. That summer, I painted more than 24 watercolors on Damariscotta Lake, on the rocks at Casco Bay, and from Sullivan Street in Portland, Maine.

Another interesting thought entered my mind then, too. I should return to school to find a new career. I looked into classes at the University of Maine, but the thought of shoveling snow in winter was intimidating. I didn't know how.

I returned to Maui Community College in 1997, and in 2000 I received a BA in Liberal Arts from the University of Hawai'i. I received the Lena Chang Award from the Nuclear Peace Foundation in Santa Barbara, California. It was a large scholarship that helped pay for living expenses while I attended MCC. I applied for several Masters Programs, including Political Science, American Studies, and Creative Writing. I was accepted into one program, immediately.

Three weeks after our UH graduation, I started the program at Middlebury College's Bread Loaf School of English. It is a school for writers and the teaching of writing, and named after a mountain overlooking the campus in the Green Mountain National Forest in Vermont. I spent the next five summers on campuses in Vermont, Santa Fe, New Mexico, Juneau, Alaska and Oxford, England. In August of 2004, I received my Masters Degree in English at Lincoln College in Oxford, England. Education was my key to a happier path.

It was during these five years that this book was written. As I wrote this manuscript, I was not aware that my project was a search for meaning and stability from my past. I just thought it might be a good story. It only occurred to me after the many re-writes and re-readings that this memoir had a purpose beyond my expectations. This memoir became its own being. It is also about the people of Orpheum Village who instilled in me the values I have today.

—Jackie Pias Carlin, May 2006. Kihei, Maui, Hawai'i

Glossary

Aieyy Apo—Filipino expression, "Oh Lord."

aku— Hawaiian name for skipjack fish

armang—Japanese dried fish

bacalao—Filipino dish with codfish derived from the Spanish.

bango—Number tag used by workers for Identification in the sugarcane and pineapple companies.

banyo—Outhouse or outside toilet.

Barong Tagalog—Filipino dress shirt

Bataan Death March—War crime in the Philippines committed by Japanese Forces in 1942.

battikulen—Filipino word for chicken gizzard

Bell House— Small office and meeting station for plantation workers in Pa'ia.

biagan – Filipino word used for cockfight. However, I could not find the same definition in the Filipino dictionaries. It is possibly a Hawaiian Creole word derived from the following words: bulang – cockfight; bulangan – place of cockfight). (Many thanks to Lito Artates and Merlino Fetalvero for explaining that the word biagan does not exist in the Filipino language. However, I found the following meaning on the Internet: *biagan* – Ilocano word for lively; to enliven. Possibly Hawaiian Creole word derived from the followinging words: *bulang*—cockfight; *bulangan*—place of cockfight.

bumbye—Hawaiian Creole word for "by and by".

cabatete—squash

chop suey—Pidgin English word mixed vegetables with meat dish

chicken hekka—local variation of Japanese sukiyaki

chicken skin—goose bumps; chills

Dahil Sa Iyo—modern Filipino love song

ebi—Japanese dried shrimp

Filipino—Language or people of the Philippines

Gandule—Puerto Rican word for pigeon pea

haku lei—Type of Hawaiian lei

hanafuda—Japanese card game

hānai—Hawaiian word for adopted

haole—Hawaiian word for newcomer, normally not used derogatorily.

haole koa—Hawaiian name for a bush resembling koa.

Hawaiian Creole—Hawaiian Pidgin English created by immigrants based on the Hawaiian language structure, and now the common language among locals.

Hongwanji—Japanese Buddhist mission

hula—Hawaiian ancient and modern dance

Ilocano—Philippine region and dialect

iriko—Japanese dried fish

Kā‘ana-pali—Area in West Maui

kālua—Hawaiian roast in a ground pit

kama‘aina—Hawaii‘an native born person

kau kau—Chinese word for food

kau kau tin—Aluminum receptacle that stored lunches. There were usually two compartments, one stacked on the other, with a cover and a handle.

kukū—Hawaiian word for thorn or burr.

Spirit of the Village

kirog—Filipino word for stir frying rice. (Merlino
Fetalvero explained this to me, although my father
used this word to show me how to clean rice).

kiawe—Hawaiian word for Algaroba Tree. Thorny tree
found at the beaches and used for firewood.

kimono—traditional Japanese clothing

Lahaina—Historic Town in West Maui

lai—Hawaiian fish

lanai—Hawaiian word for balcony or patio

lau hala—Hawaiian word for Pandanus. Used for
weaving mats, hats, and other items.

Launiupoko—Area in West Maui

liliko'i—Hawaiian word for passion fruit

limu—Hawaiian word for seaweed

luna—Hawaiian word for foreman

mabuhay—Filipino salutation for long life

malihini—Hawaiian word for long time resident of
Hawai'i

manang—Filipino word for female older than the
speaker.

manong—Filipino word for male older than the speaker.

make—Hawaiian word for "to die".

māhū—Hawaiian word for male with feminine
characteristics.

marunggay— Filipino vegetable. Marungae. Oil of Ben.
Leaves and seed pods are edible.

Maui hot dogs—the very best of red hot dogs on Maui
during the 50s.

mua—Hawaiian word for before, or first

nakkong—Filipino word for child.

obake—Japanese word for ghost.

obi—Japanese fabric belt used with kimono

O Bon—Japanese event honoring their ancestors

Olowalu—Area on the west side of Maui before Lahaina

ō'io—Hawaiian bonefish

'opihi—Hawaiian sea limpet

payut—Filipino card game similar to Poker

pali—Hawaiian word for cliffs above the ocean

palanggan—Filipino word for large pan

pāpio—Hawaiian fish. Baby ulua.

paria—Filipino word for bittermelon. Filipino vegetable. Leaves and fruits are edible.

patis—Filipino fish sauce. Also used in Thai and Vietnamese dishes.

pau— Hawaiian word for finished or completed.

pau hana—Hawaiian for "finished with work".

Pele—Hawaiian goddess

Poi—Hawaiian staple made from taro

Portagee—Pidgin English for Portuguese

pūnāwai—Hawaiian word for water spring. We used it in terms of the pond and ditches that brought water to the sugarcane fields.

pune'e—Hawaiian word for couch.

Rizal Day—December 31 commemorating Dr. Jose Rizal, a   revolutionist and hero of the Philippines.

romero—Filipino word for rosemary.

Single Man or Single Men—Terms used for males who came from the Philippines to work in Hawaii's sugar plantations, either bachelors or without their wives and families.

Some mo'—Pidgin English for more

Sweet Bread— Portuguese Baked Sweet Bread. Popular fundraising item.

tabis—Japanese cloth socks with a separation between the big toe and the second toe.

tansu—Japanese chest of drawers for clothing.

tata—Filipino greeting of respect to an older male.

taro— Hawaiian tuber that poi is made from.

Terno Gowns—Formal dress of the Philippines with "butterfly" sleeves.

Tournahauler—cane hauling truck

ulua—Hawaiian word for Blue Crevalle fish.

weke—Hawaiian word for yellowstriped goatfish.

Visayan—Filipino region and dialect.

Bibliography

Bartholemew, Gail. *The Index To The Maui News—1930- 1950.* Maui Historical Society, Wailuku, Maui, HI. University of Hawai'i. U.S.A. 1991.

Bartholemew, Gail. Bailey, Bren. *Maui Remembers A Local History.* Mutual Publishing 1994.

Duensing. Dawn E. *Pā'ia: Evolution Of A Community.* Pā'ia Main Street Association. 1998.

The Maui News. Strike Ends!! Saturday, June 7, 1958. p. 1. Wailuku, Maui, T.H. 1958.

The Maui News. Issues 1910-1965. Kahului Library. Kahului, Maui, Territory of Hawai'i.

Murayama, Milton. *All I Asking For Is My Body.* A Kolowalu Book. University of Hawaii Press. 1975.

Ocean Sports Distributors. *Hawaiian Reef Fish.* Chart.

PO Box 1018. Kihei, Maui, HI 96753. 1993.

Pukui, Mary Kawena. Elbert, Samuel H. *New Pocket*

Hawaiian Dictionary. University of Hawaii Press.

Honolulu. 1992.

Pukui, Mary Kawena. Elbert, Samuel H., Mookini,

Esther T. *Pocket Place Names of*

*Hawai'i.*University of Hawaii Press. Honolulu.

1989.

Santos, Hector. *Katalogo ng mga Apelyidong Pilipino*

(Catalog of Filipino Names) 1998. 18 November.

2005. http://www.bibingka.com/names/

Takaki, Ronald. *Raising Cane. The World Of Plantation*

Hawaii. Chelsea House Publishers. 1994.

Tanaka, Earl. *Union Reports Reaction to Meals OK;*

Some Complain. The Maui News. Wednesday, March 5,

1958. p. 1-2. Wailuku, Maui, Territory of Hawai'i.

1958.

In Memory
of
Cathie Quillope
1946-2006

Jackie Pias Carlin has lived on Maui since 1949. She has had many lives as a professional entertainer, visual artist, instructor in art, cooking, and writing. She has also taught writing at Maui Community College. She presently offers creative writing workshops in autobiography at Maui's senior centers at Kaunoa and Lahaina. Carlin and the staff at Kaunoa Senior Center publish an ongoing collection of seniors' essays, *Where Were You During World War II?*

She also publishes **Write On Maui**, an online ezine for creative writers. www.writeonmaui.com. Blog your comments or post Q&A's at http://jackiepiascarlin.maui.net, the official site for *Spirit of the Village A Maui Memoir.*

When she is not traveling, or working fulltime at her computer, Jackie takes hula classes, paddles with an outrigger canoe club, and practices ta'i ch'i.

Quick Order Form

Pay Pal Credit Card orders: http://writeonmaui.com/reserve.htm

Email orders: orders@maui.net

Postal Orders: Write On Maui, PO Box 1210, Wailuku, Maui, HI 96793 USA.

Please send the following books, or disks.

Books:_____

Disks:_____

Please send more FREE information on:
Check one or more-
     Other Books
     Speaking/Workshops
     Consulting

Name:_____
Address:_____
City:_____State:_____Zip:_____
email:_____
phone:_____fax:_____

U.S. Dollars: $14.95 per copy + 4.17% Hawai'i Sales Tax.
$ 5.00 Shipping/Handling by Priority Air within the U.S.A.
(Please convert to Canadian Dollars if ordering from Canada.)

Payment: Check   or   Credit Card: (Please circle one)
                    Visa   MasterCard
Card number:_____
Name on card:_____
Exp. date:_____